"On Consciousness - Journeys, Rituals and Meditations" is a book written by Gonzalo Bénard

This book combines the previously released books "I, Energy" and "MPower the Shaman" in their revised versions.

All copyright ©GonzaloBénard 2017

Book cover's design and all photographs and paintings included in this book are by ©GonzaloBénard

All rights reserved, including the right to reproduce this book or portions thereof in any form whatsoever.

Gonzalo Bénard
www.gbenard.com
@GWBenard

contact: gbenard@gbenard.com

About the author

Gonzalo W. Bénard is a visual artist who has been working in different media such as painting, drawing and photography, and is the author of 'I, Energy' on consciousness and shamanism, and "MPower the Shaman, a disquiet shift of Consciousness".

Born in Lisbon, from Spanish and French descendants, with a cultural background, he soon went to the Himalayas, where he spent 3 years both in a Buddhist Monastery School of Philosophy and Arts, and at the highlands spending time learning and practicing with the Shamans from the old Tibetan Bon tradition.

Being curious since a very young age and avid reader of science, sociology and culture, he has been travelling for more than 20 years mainly through Europe, Africa and Asia, also discovering other rituals and practices of shamanism.

Gonzalo Bénard is a natural born healer and shaman, practicing transcendental meditation since he was 13 years old; he took refuge in the ancient Tibetan Bon Shamanic tradition as Bonpo K. Lodro Zangpo while in the Himalayas.

by©GBénard

On Consciousness

Journeys, Rituals and Meditations

by Gonzalo W. Bénard

Δ

"The man's heartbeats are part of the
symphony on the Earth.
Everything is energy".
Nikola Tesla

Δ

Introduction:

The author went through 3 days of brain death to come back to life. He lived 3 years in Himalayas learning with old shamans and Buddhist masters, and spent some time in Africa with shamans and healers. Since a very young age he accepted and understood that he had open channels of energy; that he could use the energetic channels to heal himself and others. And that you can also open your channels to the Cosmic Consciousness.

In this book Bénard tells you how to heal, yourself and others, and how to be connected with your higher self, sharing his own journeys and experiences.

Bénard, a shaman himself following the Tibetan Bon tradition, explains all this in a simpler manner, and how the daily practice of meditation can make your life much more simple than it is. How you should listen and feel for a better life on Earth connected to the Universe.

Living in the now: feeling one with the whole.

Connected. Being energy on the same wave of frequency as the Earth.

Being yourself a Shaman and a Totem, guiding your own, connected to the collective and cosmic consciousness.

Δ

An architect once told me that he could take six months to design the handle of the main door of a house, and that he would only start the new project from there. He would go visit the land, sit down there and meditate on the handle for the main door, from where you would enter into the new house. Based on the view, surroundings, personality of the client, aesthetics, and most important: the energy. Only after he visualized the handle could he continue, and the rest of the project could take a month to design. The handle of the main door is the key for the whole.

When you arrive at someone's house for the first time there are many elements that can make you feel comfortable, or not at all. The smell is probably the first to come up, connected to our most basic senses. The scents you feel outside, and after passing by the main door, the scents you feel inside. Then comes our vision, the surroundings, and the home décor. We can also feel the energy of it. The energy of the land, place, and house. The energy of the house can impose itself upon the energy of the field. If the residents have powerful energy though, and the land not as much, they can over impose it. But sometimes it's not that easy because the power of the energy of the field depends on many other issues. Quantus Matter.

I was once invited to be juror of an international movie festival in the United States. After the festival I was invited to have a special lunch at what was supposed to be a very fancy and posh island. After half an hour of yachting we arrived at the most beautiful side of the island: an incredible hillside landscape with some huge neoclassical "white houses" spattering the green of the island. After an enchanted trekking around the island we then arrived at an empty open field with a large house-restaurant at the end, facing the ocean. As soon as we started crossing the field I started feeling weird, unwelcome, unease. My body started shaking with the frequency of the place. I was not comfortable there, but didn't want to say anything as I was a guest and they were being relentlessly kind. I really didn't feel comfortable going further, even less coming inside of that house, and the more we got closer, the worse I was feeling. I tried to keep myself calm, sending messages to my mind; telling it that was everything ok and that I shouldn't worry. We stepped in, and by the entrance I opened the door by its handle. I got an electric shock. I hated that handle. I felt that my energy was in a deep fight with the energy of the place. I hated that entrance. Not aesthetically, but the energy of the whole place was really bothering me. I opened the door, we came in and I felt slapped all over. My body went through a weird pain, and my mind started listening to screams. I led the group through the restaurant till the end so we could sit outside at the open balcony/terrace to the ocean. I felt really uneasy and uncomfortable. We sat down and the waiter brought the menu. I asked for a usual drink that exists everywhere:

    * We ran out of "that drink" sir.

Then, watching the menu I asked the only meal I could eat:

    * Sorry sir, we don't have that option anymore.

If I was already feeling that I shouldn't be there, when they told me that there was no drink and no meal I could take, I stood up, and kindly told my hosts that I was not feeling good and had to take a walk on the other side of the island. When I was leaving I couldn't take it anymore: There was this incredible energy coming from the land on which the restaurant was built that really bothered me so much that I couldn't be there. Not a minute more. The restaurant was mostly empty, and we were the only ones at the terrace. I left. The screams of people being killed that I was listening to were just too loud for me to handle them. The walk from the terrace through the restaurant till I reached the end of the field seemed to me endless in time. I felt in the middle of an actual battle, listening to people screaming and being killed, like in a massacre, visualizing the blood, throats being cut, men being thrown down, dying, screaming, agonizing, being buried alive. It was the most overwhelming experience for all my senses. I should have never had handled the door. Much less going into that place. They stayed there though, and I left, walking, feeling the soil with every step, walking away, and leaving those deathly screams behind me. I then sat down at the green fields of the other side of the island, taking a breath, connecting to earth. I sat under a huge oak there, watching the ocean, trying to focus on the pure energy of the ground, old tree and the movement of the ocean in front of me. Just relaxing and breathing. Feeling the whole. Trying to understand what happened there.

We met later on when they came back. I wasn't much able to talk, especially about that experience and just told them that I was finally feeling better and no need to worry. A few days later, already back home, I sent an email to an American friend whose brother is a historian/researcher: now that I finally had some emotional distance I wanted to understand what happened there. I told him everything I felt there in on land of that restaurant, the screams, the visualization of people being killed and buried, the aggressive energy that made me feel so unstable and uncomfortable. I wrote him all the details I still had fresh in mind.

It was shortly after when I received a stunning email from his brother. "Dear Gonzalo, I'm amazed by what you felt in that specific place, specially not knowing anything related to it. A long time ago that exact place was where two Indian tribes had a big fight, in which all of them were killed, and so the place where you felt uncomfortable and where you listened to them screaming and being killed, is the place where they were all buried. Some of them left agonizing. That land was supposed to be a sacred spot, but it was taken by other beings to build their business. I'm sure that there were more people not feeling comfortable there, or else, what was supposed to be a great restaurant would have been filled with guests. Not with huge dinning rooms empty."

That moment still remains alive, very well detailed in my bank of memories: I still see clearly what I visualized there.

Recently I was told that the restaurant was finally demolished and there's nothing on the land. Just green: and a tree growing from the ashes of the people who were violently buried there. They may now rest in peace.

There's no door handle anymore: It's now an open field connecting Earth to Heavens. No animal is to be seen there either, no birds on the green tree.

Damn handle. Damn moment that I opened the door by its handle to step over sacred land.

It amazes me though how most people are now so disconnected with collective energy that they are not sensitive anymore to places, or even to their own feelings. The old wisdom of the shamans seems to have been replaced by a commercial superficial ground.

It has been an inner battle since I was a kid: the intuition vs. logic / natural being vs. western education. In the western world we're tamed to think in a logical scientific way using only our mind. In the east, I faced what was natural to me since I know myself: intuition and consciousness. Growing up between these two different cultures we learn how to use both, as the two of them can be complementary to each other.

Usually I'm aware of my intuition and I'm able to follow it. It's not always easy though, when you live in a western urban place due to the collective mind and energy. But whenever we work out our inner silence we must be able to listen to our intuition better, as well as our own mind. I grew up working on both. I grew up with them colliding with each other. Resisting each other. Having inner battles. Learning with both. Getting annoyed when I failed one because of the other. The process is not that simple when you can't find the balance: the inner balance of mind and consciousness, of logic and intuition. But the whole process is rewarding at the end. We grow up in our own battlefield. Otherwise we don't.

"Quantus" is a Latin word that later on started being used as quantum/quanta.

It's usually used in reference to a minimum amount of energy by physicians. But it's also used in philosophy or even by mystics. Although we will not feed the arguments between the Einsteins' or Plancks' or Spinozas' of this world, I will for sure bring references of both science and mysticism. Or the use of Quantum. Or most probably the use of the Mater Energy.

A couple of years ago I was told that the South Korean art photographer Jungjin Lee was in Paris, and having an exhibition there. I contacted her and invited her for a conversation, and of that conversation I later wrote an article. During the wonderful meeting that went on for hours, she whispered to me her own creative process. Her main work is based on the wind. In fact she portrays air in the greatest way. Or in emptiness itself.
It came to my mind then the concept of emptiness by Tao: Wu. Or how Lao-tzu's disciple, Chunag-tzu described it: "The still mind of the sage is the mirror of Heavens and Earth, the glass of all things. Vacancy, stillness, placidity, tastelessness, quietude, silence, and non-action – this is the level of Heavens and Earth, and the perfection of the Tao and its characteristics."
Her artworks, in real life size, had the magic of sending me back to the eastern culture, or to breathe what I deeply felt while in a Tibetan monastery meditation state: Emptiness.

Emptiness of mind. A good damn void.

[8]
"I like the desert. I love to be in it." she says. I should have been prepared for this kind of answers she gave to me through all the conversation we had, but I guess I forgot to re-locate myself in an eastern culture and play with intuition instead of logic. How come Jungjin tells me that she likes the desert when she lives between two of the four most populated cities in the world? In fact she lives inside her own work. In her own silence. Her own desert, where she feels and lives the emptiness.

"The empty space is more important than the represented object. Like in the stage of a dance show where you have the dancer in movement: he can't move if there's no empty space around."

"The importance is not the object, but the emptiness that surrounds it".

Like a Japanese master of calligraphy brushing the soul's "thing": You must be the emptiness to create.
"I sit down, meditate and leave the Winds to go away from my mind. Then I can visualize a Thing. I focus on it. I hypnotize it. I collect its energy. And only after I get its soul I'm able to photograph it. Then, in the studio, I take all the shadows that don't belong to the Thing. And I evolve it with the emptiness that I felt in meditation, as that Thing only existed because there was emptiness of mind."

I started this morning listening to a piano concert. I grew up in a house with a grand piano and a vertical one. But the pianos there were for the women of the house. Not allowed by the boys. I used to sit down then at the rocking chair, in silence, eyes shut, listening to my grandmother playing it. Playing Chopin mostly. Or my old aunt playing some more contemporary music. One day, home alone, I sat down at the piano, put a music sheet there, and decided to give it a try. I was caught though, and sent back to my room. I never learned piano, but I turned into a listener. Every day I listen to piano, no matter at what time. Usually at night, classical, jazz or contemporary. Sometimes I take a break during the day to sit down and listen, instead of napping. Piano can easily make me go into a kind of soft trance. It connects me. Today was no exception.

A few days ago I was taking a long walk by the ocean when a flash came to my mind: suddenly I visualized the title of this book and the concept of the content. I was so in awe that I didn't take note… and forgot.

Today, while morning "coffeeing" to awake the mind, listening to Jan Lisiecki playing Bach – and crying over it -, I came into one of those soft trances. I couldn't do anything while listening to him playing. Lisiecki connects souls. He knows well where the soul of the piano is located. He feels it. He's aware of his own soul as well, and connects both in a deep, wise and sensitive way. He cries along the music that he plays. I allowed myself to go into this trance created by him. For almost two hours I was not even on Earth. When the music ended I listened to another concert of his. Suddenly, as a result of this trance, the title of the book came back to my mind, very lively with the content of the writing. It came back. I immediately wrote it down and didn't stop.

This too about emptiness. About the energy that one can use to create. To connect. In fact there are three major piano players that I use to listen more often than others. Although they're both great, or even the best, each one has a unique approach to the music, or to the instrument itself. While Jan Lisiecki finds the soul and connects causing a trance, Evgeni Kissin is a cathartic brain: he doesn't breath while playing and doesn't allow you to breathe either. Keith Jarrett, no matter if he's playing classic or jazz, uses all his tantric energy, playing the piano with a deep sexual energy. He's physically energetic.

Curious, how these three can complete the triangle: consciousness/mind/body. The balance.
And how each one can influence my writing, the flow, the rhythm or even the content of it. Once in a while – in fact quite often - I allow myself to be in silence. I use my wireless noise cancelling headphones though, so I'm in absolute silence while in the city. Listening to the void. And how much I'm able to connect with myself in these

moments. With life itself.

"Matter" is the substrate from which physical existence is derived, remaining more or less constant amid changes. The word "matter" is derived from the Latin word *māteria*, meaning material, as distinct from "mind". In ancient Greek philosophy, *arche* is the beginning or the first principle of the world. Empedocles held though that there are four elements, from which things are derived, Earth, Water, Fire and Air. Some added a fifth element, the Ether, from which the Heavens were derived. Socrates accepts that list.

"Mater" is the Latin word for mother, the beginning, where the energy is created.

When I was 7 years old I started having some arguments at school. Mainly at catechism. To the catholic teacher's approach to death I could only deeply disagree. I never understood the concept of Heaven and Hell. I told her then that when we die we would be buried as ashes and that our energy would go to another baby who would be born some time later whenever my consciousness would be ready to live in another body. My energy would then take some information that we rarely have access to unless we work on it, not in a logical/mindful way.

It was then when I became uneasy at school, as seen by the Jesuits who ran it. My visionary theories were just a product of the energy that was installed by them in my own existence. I believed in that and so it made much more sense to me. I didn't need to read anything about that, I knew it from deep inside of me.

Telepathy, teleportation, levitation, etc. were obvious to me. Since I was born I had this knowledge of being just energy. When I went through the three days of brain death I had it proven to myself.

Death is just a temporary formless concept of oneself. We fear death for several reasons, the first one being related to suffering. We do relate death with suffering, so we whish to die fast. Suffering is not something we want, and most of all because we can't control it. We can't control death either, and not being able to control is what frightens us. We spend all our lives trying to control, to have everything under our own supervision. We don't trust even when we say we do. We fear. We fear not to have control of a situation, even more when the situation is one that belongs to the unknown. We fear and we don't trust. So we have religions to make it easier to live. We need something "supreme" to make us have something on which we can project our fears, to hide under ignorance. Yes, it's easier. We then follow the ones we take as supreme so we can find some support. The faith. The blind faith that makes you believe in every single dogma. Religion, nowadays, is not that different in concept from the old mythologies though. They didn't know what could cause a storm, so they created a god for storms, adjusted to the different cultures, to blame them, to justify it, to make us believe that there's nothing we can do about it. They didn't have any plausible scientific knowledge. It was just a matter of time to have the religions organized. As yet another pyramid of power. Like politics. Like corporations. But we do exist as individuals, even though we tend to be afraid of being one. We do exist as a body, a form of energy. Or going further, as a triangle of energies: body, mind, and consciousness. Christianity knows it and gives to the world that triangle: God, Christ and Spirit. All energy in different shapes. In one, to be feared. Plato was right when he describes humanity as living in a cave thinking that the shadows were the light so we don't have to seek for the light itself. I heard that some people go out from there though.

Talking with people, keeping a conversation, is something that tires me immensely. Although I know it's important, and sometimes I even get loose on that as if it was natural to me. Natural to me is to remain in silence. Or to think out loud to listen to my own voice just as a facility to organize thoughts. Not to be answered, even less to make a conversation.

A curious fact though is that since society has imposed upon us that we should communicate and express – under its own standards – we feel that need. We even learn foreign languages so it would make easier to communicate and express with a wider population. If I think out loud in Portuguese, French or Spanish amongst a group of only English speakers I might not be understood, so I learned English. Is that really necessary? By my own experience, no. But then, yes, if we want life to be lived easier. Or more acceptable within society.

Telepathy is harder to achieve in a more superficial/logical environment. However, it does make much more sense to me. Telepathy is a form of communication that knows no boundaries, no limits or barriers of one language. The now world is getting it back. Or going forward with that. On one hand there's internet connecting people making the whole population to learn only the main languages: English / Spanish / Chinese. On the other hand the geographic cultures, countries, are getting even more divided by languages. In Europe for example.

Spain has Cataluña imposing the use of the once lost Catalan, Country Bask writing down Euskera, which was only verbal, Galicia being proud of Galician… in a country where everybody ends up speaking Spanish. Or even in smaller countries like Belgium or Switzerland, with their three official languages.

When I was living in Barcelona I had daily (small) talks with the lady who run the café-bar in front of my house. She's a proud Catalan and would only speak Catalan. I was not that familiar with the language though, so I would speak only in Spanish. Even though I started reading Catalan newspapers and being more familiar with their language somehow I kept talking to her in Spanish. For 7 years we had daily conversations: she in Catalan, me in Spanish. We did understand each other. We made an effort to understand each other: oneness, rather than separateness. Most of the time, whenever I wanted to say something deeper in Spanish that she couldn't understand, I would send the information through telepathy so she would get it even not knowing how. I often connected with her through telepathy to ease the communication. She never knew that.

Telepathy is a form of communication from consciousness to consciousness. It's quantum communication. We think, therefore we communicate. We communicate, therefore we express. But the moment we try to put it in words we will find barriers. Take for example the knowledge of Chinese, who use logograms instead of alphabet. Logograms represent a word, in contrast with phonograms, which represent sounds. Logograms are what we commonly call ideograms, so whenever you write down a Chinese character, you're designing an idea. If you want to say "fight", you would draw a character representing a fighter mirroring another. Or take the example of "moonlight":

they would represent the "sun" next to the "moon" character, which means that the moon is being visible due to the sunlight over it. This makes that Chinese need to know a lot more ideograms to express. But it's also a matter of logic: if you know how to represent a fighter, you know how to write "fight". We have it easier though: we have one letter per each sound. Even though some sounds that exist in Portuguese, one of the most complex and complete languages from Latin, like French, don't exist in other languages. For this reason is also good to know different languages as we can describe something in a different one, whenever ours doesn't have what we want to say.

"L'esprit de l'escalier" is an example, being a French saying used by other cultures, like English. It means the predicament of thinking of the perfect answer when it's already too late for it. So many times we leave a conversation to go back home and find the right answer we could have given.

We do get lost with words. We get lost trying to say the right word, to structure the right sentence, to describe the event the most accurate way, often enlarging stories to make it more real.

Using telepathy is what it is. We have the idea or event in mind and we allow its transmission through energy empathy. From one consciousness to another.

For westerners the main problem or the difficulty in understanding this is just due to the overdose of conscious thought that our mind has been programmed to do. Plus: the collective thought.

If you travel alone and allow yourself to be open to the new cultures you might notice something interesting. I can only relate to my own travels though. And if you're not aware of your own self, or do not have a strong personality – or have a closed one – you might not feel it. Whenever I'm in Portugal I feel a collective energy of low self-esteem that can only create boundaries in one's need of pursuing a richer level of knowledge. People get stuck, afraid of being themselves, and you feel that you're stuck as well. That you can't go further.

In Paris the collective energy is deeper, you feel the weight of culture, you feel the need to base your thoughts, you read the French philosophers and writers like Sartre or Camus. You take walks in the *Cemitière du Père Lachaise* and you feel the need to go even deeper. There is this collective awareness that makes you enjoy your own loud thoughts in inner silences, your living brains wired. The opposite of Spain, in which you feel a superficial freedom, a collective energy of freedom, of shouting the unthinkable and unbased often biased thoughts.

The same happens not only with culture but also with time.

Our own concept of time differs from place to place, from collective energy to collective awareness. When you're in Africa you feel time in a different way then when you're in a big city no matter if you are in Europe, or Japan. Most of the time we are not even aware of it, because we think that it is us who have changed, when we are just being caught by the collective energy, that is shared with us through empathy, through telepathy, straight to our consciousness, and finally from our consciousness to our mind. Filtered.

If you ever have gone to a hypnosis session you should know this. First you need to find a therapist with whom you feel trust and respect. Then go for it with a question. And an open mind.

When the session starts, the therapist gives you instructions on how to stop it in case you feel uncomfortable, so you can have total control of the whole process. This is very important, as I said before we do have this need of control. Over everything. Including over our own self. The session then starts: when you're going under hypnosis what happens is that the therapist will put your mind asleep and bring out the consciousness.

Our mind has filters. It knows what makes us suffer for example. The mind is the one that decides if and when it gives you access to the memory bank. It happens often that someone who goes through a traumatic experience has some difficulty in visualising it afterwards, or even expressing it.

So the memory gets freed, and you do need to be able to digest whatever comes out of you. This is why it is important to trust your therapist and follow their guidance: there are many things in your own life that you're not aware of: unless you know how to decode your consciousness.

When I did a specific session of self-hypnosis I went to the moment in which I was born, and I could describe my birth accurately. I then told it to my father and he confirmed, saying that was impossible for me to remember that. I do remember my birth. All of it. Including the first face I saw in this world: the face of the doctor, who died few weeks later. He was an English man, tall, bald and with blue eyes. The first face I saw, when coming out from a woman's "guts".
It is such a traumatic experience that no one remembers it though.

I'm now sitting writing this, drinking a white tea with ginger, listening to Bach on my noise cancelling headphones so I'm fully disconnected from the world. I know that there are people in the house though. And suddenly I'm craving for a couple of dates. Not like Dali who liked dates to get that sticky thing to keep his moustache erected. I like eating dates.

In my mind I'm thinking how nice it would be to have a couple of dates now to enjoy. I visualised one of the people in the house with this in mind. I sent this visual energy to that person: dates. A visual picture of dates transmitted through telepathy. It shouldn't take more than 2 minutes for that person to think of dates, go get some from the kitchen and come to me to ask if I want some.

Three minutes was what it took though. She just brought me a bowl of dates. She got the telepathic message, a wireless connection that exists between us: people, animals, or plants.

However, if you decide to not follow your instincts, you first think of dates (as intuition thought that goes from your consciousness to your mind), and then you rationalize and think: "hmm… why did I think of dates? There's also figs, so I can bring them instead." And then you fail, because you didn't follow your instinct, just your rational mind. Your instincts are brought to you by your consciousness, which is way deeper and wiser than your mind. Even if you don't think so. Or even if you're afraid to listen to it.

You might have noticed that sometimes when you go in a place you feel your mood change. The energy of the place is different from yours. Or just different from the one outside. Maybe because there's someone who has stronger energy and changes the whole environment. And you feel stressed, suddenly, out of the blue. Or completely relaxed, depending on the collective energy.

In Barcelona, a stressful city, I often had friends coming over, and most of the times I heard them saying: your house is like an island, as if all the stress was left outside. A shrine, or a sacred temple in which we can absorb and recycle our anxieties and worries. Some of my friends would go there just to feel relaxed. To breathe. Sometimes they would just come for a nap to be near me while I was painting.

Each one of us is an abyss. With clear skies above and deep darkness bellow, so you can fly up or fall down. Some people just levitate though. This was what I felt and visualised during the period of coma before my brain death. Without any concept of a physical body.

I don't like going into a conversation. I do often talk and listen, but not necessarily to keep a conversation going, as in a dialogue. If I express any thought, I don't expect anyone to follow it and continue with it because I'm not expecting answers. When I talk, what I'm doing is just expressing my thoughts out loud, most of the times directly from my consciousness. I notice it more when I'm giving interviews. With writing it is the same: I express my thoughts, from my consciousness to the words on paper. Whenever I lose a part of what I wrote I have no memory of it.

When I wrote "The Sacred Book of G", I didn't read it. When I finished the book I had no idea of what I wrote. Only after it was published, when I had it in physical form on paper in my hands, did I read it and was finally able to know what was in it. Writing, as is talking, are more than ways to express: they are ways to release. To turn our thoughts into something organised, and conscious, and logical.

Quite often this happens to autistic people. We're naturally non-verbal. Not that we don't know how to talk, or even less that we don't understand. We just don't find the need to waste energy talking. We do understand, sometimes even more than others. We feel it. We are focused on that. But we don't feel the need to keep a dialogue, unless there's a direct question to be answered. We might assume that the other person said what they had to say and that is all. We listen and we talk whenever we feel the need to. Most of the time we don't. We can express it through different ways, like drawing, dancing or writing. Writing doesn't have a dialogue, it's our mind put into written words. Maybe we even have the sounds in our mind, but more often we have the visual of the word, or the content of it. We can be great telepaths because we're visual thinkers. Most of us I guess. Being non-verbal we can focus better on the way we absorb. The same happens with stimming, a way to keep the balance or give rhythm to our own thoughts. You can see this happening in some classes of some cultures. For example if you see the students in a Muslim school you might see them rhythmically balancing while reading the Quran. Or in Tibet, reading the sacred mantras. Being a pendulum. Finding the inner balance. Creating energy with streams of thoughts. Stimming, finding balance can be very mind stimulating. Even if it can be annoying to others, stimming is natural and irrigates the brains bringing balance to oneself. Being a pendulum can also be a natural way to produce energy while getting focused.

I lived in the Himalayas for a few years, in a region between Nepal and Tibet. Even though my main base was a school monastery of philosophy, painting and martial dance, I often went trekking through the mountains. In fact I remained there in the high mountains for several months, for few different occasions, with different purposes. One of them was solely to meditate: to find silence within me. I had just arrived there and I needed that time alone to silence the western mind. Another time was to meet with Tibetan shamans, so I could learn and practice with them. Meanwhile I also spent some time in a lost monastery in the mountains, learning with a Buddhist master, an important Rinpoche. I also trekked to some interesting places where I went through amazing energetic experiences.

Even though I have worked with energies since a very young age, it was in the Himalayas that I found the "How to", or even realised that working with energies can give you the most basic and elementary answers… some of them to hard questions we get through our lives.

There, during my journey, I wrote a few diaries, trip journals, which I kept, secretly. Curious to read them now again after so much time back in urban western jungles. In fact I'm tempted to share with you some of those encrypted writings from my journals.

But let's focus on sacred places. No matter to which religion the sacred place belongs, the temples use to have a special energy. All of them. In my journeys I've been to Catholic and Protestant Churches, Buddhist and Hindu Temples, Jewish Synagogues and Islamic Mosques. All of them have their own special energy and you noticed that for sure. And the older they are the more impact they have in their energetic field. Even in open sacred places, no matter if Fatima or Stonehenge, sacred or pagan. In closed underground ones too, like old catacombs. You feel the energy of the place, an energy that you can't find in regular buildings. Why is this happening? Why do we feel attracted to that silent energy? Even if we're atheists we can feel it. I do too. These places have been around forever, and since people are always attracted to them, to pray, to cry within themselves, to hope, to be grateful. The message used to be good, hopeful, and grateful. People don't throw away their energy talking: they pray in silence, they listen to their inner self, they pray for others. They find hope and gratitude. And when you have a place in which people go to pray, to feel hope, silence and gratitude, the energy remains and you can feel it. It's the energy that people leave and share that makes a place sacred. Or the opposite, if you go into a temple in which they perform "satanic" rituals, you might feel confused at least. In the new temples, or in the temples of the new religions you might not feel anything. Go to one and you might feel nothing, an innocuous energetic field. Like in a lab without the smell of the chemicals. Go to a hospital and you will feel a completely different mood and energy.

I'm very sensitive to energies, so going to a hospital is always a very draining experience. Recently I had to go to one to take a relative for a treatment. While I was sitting there waiting, I was feeling all the diseases from those people in the waiting room. I knew what each one of them had. I looked at one and I felt a pain in my stomach, at another and I felt the pain on my back, on my head, on my foot. In the hospitals the energy is not linear and can be very confusing. Even if you go to a chapel in there. Hospitals use to have a chapel, not with images, just a silent room so you can be in silence, no matter to which God you pray or believe. It's a silent place, a white room that they call chapel. Usually it is an innocuous place. No energy, just silence. People don't go there to pray, they go to find silence. To take a breath while they're in the hospital. It's not a sacred place. It's just a silent one.

Each place has the energy left by the people who go there. Some of them had millions of people through the years: praying, being grateful or searching for hope. This is what makes a place sacred. The communication between life and death. An energetic communication in communion between souls. Between the Earth and Heavens.

But do it yourself if you never went to one: go visit a XIII century church, and go visit a modern temple. You will be astonished by the difference of energy in each of them.

As in the experience I went through in the Native Indian battlefield, the energy of the living beings and souls who were there is unique. Each one left a bit of themselves behind. The ground absorbs as much as the stones of which the walls were built. The wood of their doors and even the imagery inside. The people who were buried underground. As in most old churches, they often have catacombs and crypts.

If you open your energetic channels you will feel it. No matter on which ground you stand. And when you feel the energy, your consciousness will send a report to your mind informing you what's in there. You might not enjoy the experience or on the contrary you might love being there. You will stay longer or you will run away sooner. Your whole body will be informed about what you feel in there. Have you ever see a scan of your temperature during different stages of moods showing different colours when you feel more relaxed or more anxious? We change our body's heat with the feelings of the energy of places.

Take haunted houses for example, and yes, I heard a lot "I don't believe in ghosts… but I would prefer not to go in". When I came back from the years in Tibet I decided to "occupy" an old (abandoned) house of my family in the countryside. The house is very special and by what I know none of my ancestors lived there. Just for you to have an idea, the house is located in a very small village of 700 people, maybe 1.000 by now. Everybody knows each other. This house was built with a difference of 100 years: the ground floor was dated from 1610 and the first floor is more "contemporary": 1712, as it is written at the huge chimney. The whole house, when I arrived there had no kitchen inside, or even bathrooms. It had no electricity either. The first floor rooms had huge dome ceilings, and the three chimneys were those big ones with stone benches inside so you could sit by the fire. The house is beautiful. When I arrived I built a kitchen and a bathroom in two of the seventeen rooms and I also put electricity in the main ones. I chose different spaces so I could keep the house aired making me go from one side to another, to live in the whole house. From my bedroom on the first floor facing the back yard, and from my studio/office on the same floor facing the other side. From my reading room to the room with the fireplace to the west, from the kitchen downstairs next to the bathroom facing the backyard as well, and from the reception room where I eventually gave private classes to the opposite side next to the main door.

When I arrived there though, I started having people watching and wondering about me. It was the first time those people saw the house being lived in after so many years. By human beings, I mean. And only after few weeks, when they saw that I was there to stay, they approached me. I didn't understand why every one refused to work there at the beginning, as I needed the house clean, building work done, etc. It was very difficult to convince anyone to help me with what had to be done. While everybody was very sympathetic with me, no one dared to enter the house. One day I decided to meet the people in the café and straight forward I asked them why.

"The house is haunted", they all said. And if I was still there it was because I was some kind of witch. As clear as water. No one ever dared to live there. Except me.

Yes, the energy of the house can (still) be a bit chilling. The main walls are one meter thick and made of stone. I felt that the house was special ever since I was a child, going there once per year with my father to check and air the house. One of the details of the house that always made me curious was a 2mx1m stone slab on the floor in front of the main fireplace, downstairs with a view to the backyard. That stone was obviously a tombstone, or more accurately a tomb slab. Like those you find in old churches, on the floor, with scriptures in Latin, sometimes with coats of arms engraved. Even though the whole floor is made of large stone slabs, that one always made me look twice, and whenever I was turning my back to it, I often looked backwards as I felt a weird presence from there. Talking about it with my father he told me the same, that he was sure the stone was a tomb slab. Recently, the year before my father died he went there with some people to take it out, but he never told me what he found in there: "You wouldn't want to know. The slab is back into place again." I didn't ask further as he seemed quite stressed answering with these two sentences. I believe that he found more than he ever expected.

In the old times people were often buried without the certainty of their death, people in coma for example were thought to be dead, so they would be buried. And this happened quite often, so it is normal when people nowadays open old tombstones, graves, crypts, catacombs or mausoleums to find "dead" people in awkward "living" positions… since they ended up dying inside their own grave, waiting for someone to rescue them. This kind of death brings terrible energy to the place. And even though I felt good – although aware – in most parts of the house, it was difficult for me to sit by that fireplace… or to be in the bedroom upstairs. As if there was a column, a pillar of energy from the ground to the Heavens, which was not supposed to be interfered with. The bedroom right above the tomb slab was empty, and I kept the door closed. It was the only room I never opened or used. Except one day that I felt I should do something, opened the door, put some candles all over the floor, burned incense and drew all over the walls: people dancing, like Matisse's painting "*La Danse*". In a circle along the walls of the room, dancing united.

Once, I went to bed with one thought in mind: that I read somewhere, something, by someone, which made a click in my mind. Something that was not only important but also vital. So basic that I felt it was obvious, but a sort of obvious that hadn't come into my mind before: it was too basic. It was a vital thought, damn it. And as always I forgot it. I am sure it remained in my consciousness because when I read it I had that in mind: this is it! Then, I fell asleep. I didn't get worried with not remembering it because I knew that it was important enough for me to have assimilated the main thought of it. Something I read somewhere by someone had made a vital click that could change my life, or the attitude towards life itself. As humans we should always be eager and humbly open to listen and to learn. I had learned something quite important yesterday. Something, somewhere by someone. Have no idea where, what or who. But the main idea remained in my mind.

This happens a lot after my brain death. Before that, I was a living encyclopaedia and I would know and remember everything. I didn't have most of them in my front memory, but in my back bank of memories, in my consciousness' archives. It was just normal and recurring to get it back whenever I wanted. Now, I register the feeling, the concept, the essence… but not the whole. I had no clue where I read it, who wrote it or what it was. But I do remember the essence. That is what remains.

Sometimes we do tend to complicate life. We always go for the complicated quantum equations instead of paying attention to natural and basic details. I used to say that I can't stand the basic as it doesn't bring knowledge, but in fact, basic people are often the happiest in their own way of being alive. They do find answers to their quests in an easier way, as they don't go deeper into them, because they don't need to. We have this task much more complicated.

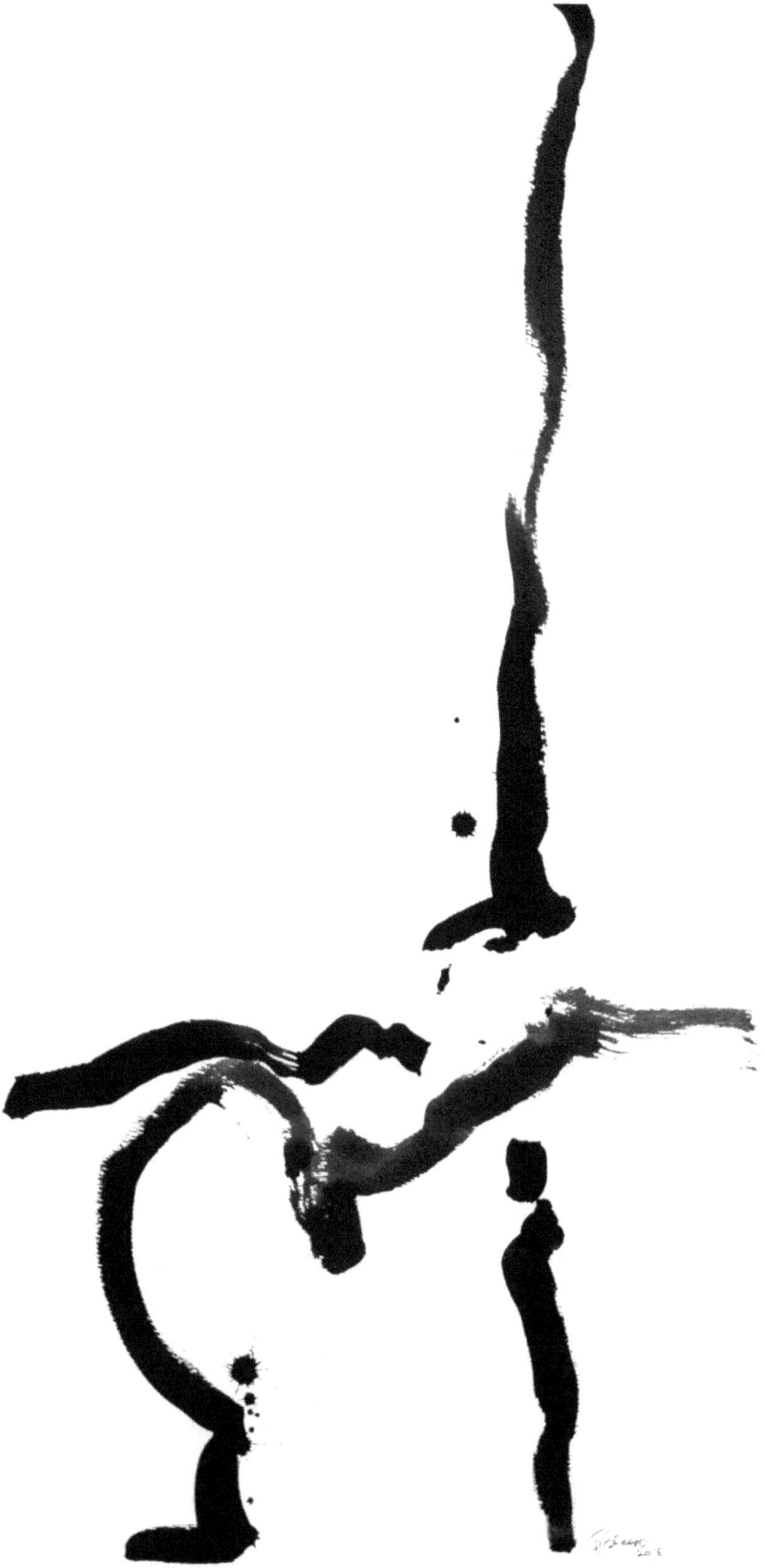

My father used to laughingly tell me that I would always have a problem in life: I would always be an optimistic seeker of knowledge, as I always find something new to fulfil me for few moments that will vanish fast because I absorb it quick enough to go on to another quest and another and another. That I would always be unsatisfied, unstoppable and hungry for knowledge like any visionary.

I still hear him laughing, happily, with his achievement. I would always be unsatisfied searching for more, as a life of challenge. So I would always have to dare myself, to live in a battlefield, to seek for wisdom as my main quest in life. To reach something that I will never be able to reach: wisdom. Wisdom is as an infinite open field, as cosmos seems to be. We will never be able to fulfil ourselves. There's no perfection whatsoever. There's no absolute truth anywhere. There's learning, quests, goals to reach. And life is just a collection of these moments of learning, challenging oneself.

We are the only ones who can change and grow up from the inside. We must by all means be able to keep standing on our feet so we can later change what surrounds us. Even though we can change others we do need to be open and humble enough to understand, learn and change ourselves.

Sometimes from the basics. It's so important to listen to basic people with no aspirations to be intelligent: they can teach us the most astonishing things. They can even make you understand how it is to be alive, as humans. As a body of energy: in a collective and universal energy.

Even though everybody - who knows me - says that I would have been a great father, and I'm conscious that I'm a good tutor, I never wanted to have children or even be with someone for life. I do enjoy my solitude, my freedom so I can go through life learning and share without being attached to anyone. Maybe it's the autistic in me who never had the need of being attached to anyone. Not that I'm anti-social, I'm not, but I usually prefer to remain in solitude with my dogs, reading, writing, travelling and meeting random strangers or once in while having deep conversations with someone who matters in that moment of space and time. With whom I can learn, or even teach something. But I guess that I learn more often than teach. Or maybe I teach a lot and I'm not even aware of it. That might happen too. Yes, frequently, I'm aware of that.

But then… I'm a creator. And I've always been a creator. I create on a daily basis as a need, vital need of living. I paint, draw, sculpt, photograph, write, cook, build. I need this to remain emotionally stable. What would have happened if instead of creating things I had created people? If I had children to raise now? Children would have been a (shared) creation, and when you create something or someone you automatically have an emotional link to it.

I spent all my life playing in several fronts. On one hand, creating art, that even though I create feeling it honestly, it has been always my main source of income: my art creations. I sell what I create to be able to live. But being a creator, or creating as an act, can be very emotionally unstable. You create as a need to express and thus it gives you emotional stability, however you end up living by it, selling the artworks you created, and what is supposed to be your work is also your emotional release. You're attached to it and you feel like you are selling your emotions. This can even make you feel lost because you feel like you are selling your most sacred and intimate side. And then you might get extremely confused: if people don't buy your work, it's because they don't like you. And this can't be more wrong. If people don't buy your work is because they don't feel connected to what you expressed, to the aesthetics of it, or because they simply don't have enough money to invest in it as artwork. It's as simple as that. It's nothing against you as a person. In fact there are lots of artists and authors who are the most awful people and their work is something that you long for. Or the opposite: it can be the most wonderful person and his creations can mean nothing, as they don't know how to express. How to communicate.

At one point when I was not very secure about my new work I felt that people were not understanding me because they were not buying any of my work. But the truth was that I was not allowing people to buy them, to own my creations because I was still very attached to them. They were my own creations, my own children. Even if I created them as a means of expression, as a need to communicate I didn't cut the umbilical chords. I didn't set them free. But that posture of not understanding the basics was driving me insane because I was not selling enough to survive: or people were not buying enough of my work.

Let's see it again: my work is very good and I'm aware of it. They are honest, they have incredible energy, people love it, and they have great quality, because I'm very demanding of it as well. So what's wrong? Why was I not selling them? Basic. I was emotionally attached to them so I created a link to my consciousness, an energetic field that didn't allow others to break in and take them: it just allowed people to see them from the other side of the energetic shield I created around the art works. After that I became anxious because I needed to sell them, and so even worse, because not only had I created a protective shield, now I was projecting my own anxiety towards the potential clients. And no one likes to feel slapped with other's anxiety. Anxiety is nothing else than energy that blocks whatever it is related to. It feels like despair, and no one likes the energy of despair.

Another thing was happening, and now I took it as a challenge, one more. Some people got closer as friends. They even loved my artwork as well, so it was great, I could not only have them as friends but I also found I could communicate with them through my creations. But then something weird happened. Whenever I gave them one of my artworks they disappeared. Something that made me feel that they were just being friends, or being close to get one of my creations. The moment they got one they would disappear. And the moment I realised that I stopped giving my own creations away. I made this a fact: every time I would give some part of me, any of my emotional created artworks, I would lose a friend. And the friends who remained as good ones never asked for one work, or they would buy them without even arguing about the value of them. Curious thing this is. The ones who got them for free disappeared; the ones who bought them remained as friends.

There is an exchange. For the former ones I was giving myself without anything in return, to the later ones there was an exchange. And in life there must be always an exchange of energies. Also, I had to learn how to detach myself from my work. And whenever I gave them away, I didn't detach, because there was nothing in return.

The return is what detaches me from them.

I have been seeing my creative works as my own children.

For work I had in mind the regular ordinary jobs, 9 to 5, in which there's a boss who pays you monthly. With creative work that I always did by myself there was nothing of this: the work was blended with emotion. It was part of my being, it was emotionally attached. Only to be detached whenever a "boss" aka client would pay for them. Then, the work was no longer mine. Till someone pays the right value for it the works are still my own, belonging to my own emotional being. And this was what made me not sell well for some time. It was what created anxiety in me, projecting despair onto others. Making it a vicious circle: no matter how good my works were I was not selling them because I was projecting anxiety and despair along with them.

One day I read something, somewhere, written by someone that clicked in my mind and changed my attitude completely. Something very basic. So basic it is obvious. But sometimes the basic is not that obvious and we do need someone, most probably a stranger, to come up with it, randomly, out of the blues, when you least expect it. My work is not me. I can be the creator of it, but as I cook/eat/poo I must let it go the moment I create it, the moment I share it with others creating the triangle between the creator – artwork – viewer, to close it as another triangle artwork – client – payment.

The same happens with my lectures or shamanic practices and healing. As we went from manuscript letters to emails, we also went from medieval markets in which you would ex-change a lamb for one rabbit and two chickens, to the use of coins, and later on to bank cards and online transfers. So any of our work got a value in the exchange process, and there must be no shame about dealing with this exchange. People exchange. It's part of life. And somehow for some time I felt ashamed of doing so: I felt that selling an artwork or any of my creations for money was like selling a son or even myself. But in fact I do my creative work not only as way to express, to communicate, but also as something that can make people proud of having them, looking at them, owning them. Like when you buy a book from an author, you pay for it and you end up getting much more. In the book in which I read those lines that changed my thoughts and attitude towards life, what I paid for was nothing compared to what I learned from it. And how often does that happen with a book: a single book can make us travel geographically or even in time. And with an artwork: whenever you purchase an artwork that speaks to you, you often find yourself lost in thoughts or going further, allowing yourself to absorb the energy of it. How often did I look at any of the artworks of my collection and found the answer I needed when I felt lost? Quite often, if you allow yourself to travel and feel the energy of them.

I remember buying a lamp, an ordinary lamp that I needed

to have by the sofa that I use to read and stretch my legs. I came back home with the new lamp and mounted it. When I finished I looked at it and suddenly I had the vision of all the people who worked for that moment of mine: from the person or people who created and designed it, the ones who invented electricity cables, the ones who worked at the electric company, the ones who created and built the bulb, the ones who built the lamp, the ones who packed it. So I can have light at night for me to be able to read. And that thought made me feel grateful to all these people who made it possible for me to have that light.

Or when I'm cooking, picking up a piece of broccoli and thinking about the conditions that the farmer had to go through to grow it into a healthy plant, the people at the market who carried it and spent the whole day there so I could buy it, cook it and finally enjoy it. A need we have to keep us alive. And I can only be grateful to all these people.

And all these. All life itself is an exchange of energy. Of energies. We are energy, we share it, but to be able to have and share we need the other part to have it as well, and exchange it with us.

When I create an artwork or write a book I'm using my own energy and the collective energy, and when I finish and share it with the world, I'm also relying on the same collective energy, to get feedback, to sell it, for others to purchase it, to enjoy it, to live it, to go deeper into it. As I purchased that lamp to use it and give me joy, others purchase my artworks and books to give them the joy they need. It's a fair trade of energy.

We just have to let go, to let life flow.

The moment I finish creating, the artworks or the books are no longer mine, they are no longer emotionally attached. I release them to the world to be consumed and purchased and enjoyed by others.
This was what I learned from that bit that was written somewhere by someone: it's an independent artwork; it's not you anymore. As when you give birth to a child and put him in the world, that child is no longer yours. It's a new life, with his own path. My artwork and books were created to be independent, to go their own path, to give pleasure and fulfil the needs of others who purchased them with their free will, in a fair trade.

Once I read something, somewhere, written by someone: the moment you create something it's no longer yours.

[42] You gave life to it yourself, so you must allow it to be owned by others. It would be selfish to keep them to yourself, and it wouldn't be fair if you kept on being emotionally attached to something that was purchased by others, thus not yours anymore. Your work is just that: something you create and make for the pleasure of others. Let them purchase and enjoy it while giving you a medium so you can keep creating and producing. It can never be personal. Everything is energy and must flow. Everything you create must go and be exchanged. It's life itself. Your mother gave birth to you and let you go after feeding you for 9 months. After birth you no longer belong to her. As none of your artworks do after the moment you shared them with the world, to be purchased. For the joy of others.

Triangles of energy create spirals of energy, in which everything should flow.

A new side table just arrived in the house. A small table made of wood from Tanzania that someone brought in. The top of it is concave, not plain straight, and it has 3 solid and beautifully carved legs. In fact it seems that the whole table, top and legs, were carved from only one piece. It's elegant yet strong.
The moment I brought it inside the house the dog started barking at it. Barking at the dark wooden table because he noticed something was in it. Dogs perceive energy easier

than humans, and that's common sense, but I was busy carrying it inside and didn't have time to check it properly. Also it's very heavy, so my whole attention and focus was to not let it fall on my feet. Or even on the floor to not damage it. I put it next to the sofa, which I use to sit to read at night, and left the room. That night, rearranging or redecorating the room, I suddenly felt someone behind my back, the moment I turned my back to the table. Someone was there and wanted to talk with me. I didn't ignore him, but told him that I couldn't talk with him at the moment, and would pay attention to him as soon as I finished the job, because I was not alone. He waited. Later on, now alone, I sat down and he showed up. He was a tall African man. He was killed but I didn't understand his connection with the table per se. I didn't understand if he was the one who built it, or carried it out, but somehow he was emotionally connected with the table and his death was related to it. That was not important at the moment as I immediately focused on how I could help him. His spirit travelled within the table though. Nothing weird with that, as objects can carry a human's or an animal's energies inside of them. The important was for him to be finally released, and since I have open channels to cosmic energies he could come out and show himself, asking to be released. Somehow he was chained to the table and now he's free. He then sat down at the table, smiling. He could go now. But he stayed there for a little while more.

He was grateful, enjoying his freedom and after that he told me he would protect me if I needed it.
This is what generally happens when you release someone who's in limbo, someone who dies with pending issues or even chained to the walls or to any object. When we free them, they become grateful and become loyal companions in one's life.
He was a very tall, fit young man with an incredible smile. The table is just a beautiful carved wood piece now. No one else is chained to it anymore.

It reminded me of when I found a wolf's broken skull in the surroundings of the country house. I didn't collect it because it was half destroyed already, but I did pick up one tooth, which later on I asked a jewellery designer who's a friend of mine to make a collar chain with it. When he finished the piece I left it outside for a sun day and a moon night so I could get it clear of energies. The day after, I wore it like I wear the other chains with different elements. The others are made from one piece I brought from Tibet, another piece from Western Sahara and the third is a crystal that was given to me by a shaman from the Himalayas. I found that this wolf tooth would make a perfect 4th element. It did. That night though I forgot to take the jewellery off and I ended up falling asleep with it. But that tooth was powerful. I woke up in the middle of the night sweating after a wild dream with a wolf. One of those intense vivid real life dreams from which you wake up sweating not being able to move, a lucid dream that you don't understand if you lived it, if you are actually still living it, if it was a scene from a past life or even a premonition. It was too intense and deeply real to just forget it. For three days I had different dreams with the same young wolf.

It is important when you wear pieces that you brought from other places, with other energies, to leave them out during the night. They need to rest, to find their own peace and freedom. During the night we not only free our subconscious while the consciousness is asleep, but we also recharge energies, so it's very important that your room remains in peace, clear and clean so you can have a restful night. Sleeping naked is also important.

During the day you can wear these pieces, like the crystal, the tooth, or any other object as protection or to absorb energies that you don't want, but at night you should take them off so they can clean themselves, or else they can transfer those collected energies onto yourself.

Triangles of spirals to infinity. A triangle is said to be the most balanced geometric figure, the most stable one. The pyramids even more, they represent the connection between the Earth and the Heavens. If you imagine a spiral over them then you also have infinity. Now imagine two pyramids with horizontal spirals topping them linked to each other creating a spiralling eight, or the symbol of infinity. Now going further – towards perfection -, imagine three pyramids in a triangle topped with spirals connected to each other. Like tornados of void connecting the Earth to the Universe, with their eyes on the top of the pyramids. What a powerful image to visualize and feel.

It's said that the real tops of the pyramids in Giza were made of pure gold and they are still underground, but there's still no evidence of the connection between the visible pyramids and their golden tops. A disk, which is also buried bellow the Sphinx, as theorists say? Would the disk be a spiral topped by smaller pyramids in gold? There's a fact though: they are not organized as a triangle but following Orion's constellation. But these are the ones in Giza, however you may find pyramids all over the world's most prominent old civilizations, like the Mayan civilization. And by what it seems, many theories will always exist about them, no matter if they were built by aliens or not. One thing seems to be universal: they have power, energetic power. They have this energetic aura that also attracts people. But they have also an incredible energy inside. Pyramids are sacred places no matter where they're located. The shape of a pyramid creates the balance between humans and gods, Earth and Heavens, since their birth.

A temple came to mind that has always fascinated me: the Rothko Chapel, a not religious sacred-place for contemplation: for silence. The Rothko chapel was commissioned to Rothko who painted a series of 14 paintings for it, in his hues of black. In the project you can also find a sculpture by B. Newton: The Broken Obelisk. This work is quite conceptual and has a pyramid as base of the broken obelisk, giving you the idea of absolute balance, yet fragile in its structure.

Also the recently built glass Pyramid du Louvre, designed by M. Pei in 1989. But previously to the Pyramid du Louvre, Tesla also tested the energy of the old pyramids.

When I came out from the 3 days of brain death I started a long process of self-therapy. First I had to improve myself physically and do some exercise, starting by a daily walk to bring more oxygen to the brain and muscles. I also lost all my memory and defences I had built over the years, so I had to work it out. Memory was a puzzle of missing pieces that I ended up rebuilding through transcendental meditation and self-hypnosis, since we have all the archives there in the consciousness. Defences can be more difficult as they come when we need them, facing again the same issues to rebuild them. But one thing remained that is weakening over time: migraines and cluster headaches. The initial months after brain death were a battle with migraines, possibly due to the lack of oxygen, thus blood circulation. Now they happen less often, but still happen at least once every two months. And when they come they tend to stay for three days. My latest one was yesterday. I often try to get rid of it immediately when I understand they're about to come. Usually I start seeing flashlights, feel dizzy and have light nausea and palpitations on my left eye. Then the migraine gets installed, like an iron bar crossing my head from the back of my neck to the right side of my left eyebrow. Sometimes, less often, a cluster one that blocks my nose and my eyesight. Whenever I feel I'm about to have one, and to avoid the three days of pain, nausea, dizziness, light sensitiveness, etc., I immediately try some energetic workouts. Sometimes using transcendental meditation working on energetic fields. Yesterday, as soon as I realised I was about to have one, I shut the blinds of the windows, put on my noise cancelling headphones with a good hour of binaural alpha frequency and lay down with my head rolled in the fabric of a Moroccan turban. The one I chose was black, and I rolled not as a turban but blind folding my eyes and forehead going back to my upper neck. I chose black because it's the colour that absorbs more. After this I went through meditation and focusing on the pain I sent it to the black scarf so it would absorb the migraine. It was a half an hour practice of meditation on energy. Visualizing the pain, I sent it to the fabric. Afterwards, when I felt it was gone, I unrolled the fabric and put it outside in the sun, hanging on a rope to get sunlight and wind to clean or recycle the energy in it. This method was enough for me to get rid of the migraine: visualizing the pain, sending it to the scarf, and taking it out to be recycled. When I finished my head was healed.

Not every pain is easy to get rid of with visualization though, especially our own pain. But we must be aware that when we have open channels of energy we easily get illness and diseases that are not ours. Sometimes we feel all the symptoms of illness or disease as if it was ours, and then we realise it's not, but from someone who is energetically or emotionally connected with us. I use to know from where the pain comes though, and when it happens it's great so you can focus on that person, knowing that the pain comes from them and heal the source directly. The moment the person is healed you will feel nothing again. You healed the source through energy, or energetic visualisation. Sometimes you know that the pain is not yours but you don't know where it comes from: in this case you have to focus on the energetic line until you find the source of it. You need to be empathic and follow the line of energy, visualizing it. These pains are easier to heal, since they are not real yours, they're just a reflection and you're helping the other to minimise the pain and heal them. When the pain is yours, like the case of my migraines and cluster headaches it is a bit more difficult, especially if you allow it to be installed, so the best way is to pay attention to the symptoms and get to work as soon as possible. When the pain is installed it is harder to get focused because it hurts. I learned how to feel the moment when the migraine would come, so it's easier now to get rid of it whenever it decides to pay a visit. I don't allow it to get installed in me anymore. Unless I'm caught by surprise.

When my father got ill I did the same.

"And yet their lives are longer than any human life, so that, behind the instant that passes, we have, in images, a quiet land of shrines and precious shapes" – Goldmund (from Narziss and Goldmund, Herman Hesse, 1930

A few days ago I was asked to remember a deeply happy moment in my life. I then searched for all the files in my conscious memories - and not finding a logical moment of happiness I went deeper in the subconscious where the main archives are. Because it was difficult to find, I questioned myself what happiness is. I don't understand most human feelings, so I checked the memories of animals to see if I could extract the feeling of happiness in them. No results. Or yes, maybe superficial moments of joy like the dog being brushed showing how much he likes it. Moments of joy are moments of happiness I thought. But what is happiness? How is the feeling?

I did experience some moments of joy, but these can be quite superficial, even though they can vibrate deeply within.

Is happiness related to a moment of awareness? To a moment of mind fulfilment? To a eureka moment of the mind? Or simply to a pleasure of the body? Is it the moment in which we find peace of mind? That sounds like a moment of happiness.

I can understand happiness as a moment of the mind's fulfilment or a moment of peace of mind.

When I see people laughing, sometimes hysterically, it frightens me a bit, because it looks like the laughing person is living the moment right before madness. It seems that when you laugh, especially if uncontrolled, you're in the presence of mind disturbance, which can be related to madness.

These thoughts have been haunting me in the last few days after observing someone's happiness for no apparent reason. Even though I was happy for her since it can be projected as feeling or emotion, I tried to make sense of it and understand what's behind happiness. Maybe I understand better the emotion of sadness because I lived it more often coming from others. Not that I have - but by empathy; since others can project their emotions and I can feel them by empathy. Maybe I've never been with happy people much. No, I did, but happiness never got me concerned, because it's a moment of joy so I let others live it. Whenever I feel someone's sadness I do feel it by empathy so I can heal it and send some more positive thoughts to the sad person. Empathy and knowledge of energy and frequency can be very useful to heal, as you can send positive thoughts to people with depression for example, by telepathy, consciousness to consciousness till it reaches the other's mind from within. When that happens, when the person receives the logical information in their consciousness through their subconscious it's great. This is something you can achieve through hypnosis. Or through transcendental meditation.

Peace of mind can be easily reachable through meditation, more deeply so by practicing transcendental meditation. And peace of mind can lead to happiness.
Mind fulfilment can also be reachable through learning, through knowledge, and when you reach a moment of wisdom you might feel happy, even though it's a moment. A moment: not a continuous state of happiness. The moment you feel the joy of wisdom, you immediately go for another one. So is wisdom a moment of happiness to remind us that we should keep searching for more, to keep us humble enough to understand that we want more?

For now I understand the concept of happiness as peace of mind and mind fulfilment. But that's my concept of inner happiness. I don't laugh when I reach it: I relax my mind for a moment.
When I have someone giving me a full body massage I can feel joy, but that is only possible, the body pleasure, after you reach some peace of mind as well. If, for example, you're not comfortable with the masseur or you don't trust them or you're worried about something, it will be difficult to achieve peace of mind, thus pleasure and joy. You might release some stress, some worries, and that can be enough for you. But is that real happiness?

Human feelings often seem to be very random, superficial and mind weakening. Most of them I don't fully understand, as they are not logical. I used to say that I don't understand why people cry, and that I never do. In fact I cried 7 times in my life, and although I remember the moments in which I cried, I don't fully understand or remember the feeling I had when that happened. I remember though the tears rolling down my face, the salty taste when I licked the tears as they reached the area easily reachable by my tongue, and the fact that my eyes look prettier and greener after that. I don't remember the feeling that led me to cry, but I do remember the release afterwards. Ejaculating can trigger the same feeling. In fact, two of the times that made me cry were after making love to someone. A deep Tantra sex experience with someone with whom you feel connected with can make you cry as much as ejaculate. It's a body/mind/consciousness release. You feel peace of mind and of body. It's an orchestrated moment. It can be a moment of fulfilment. But I don't relate it with happiness. More with bliss.

You can in fact find peace of mind when you go into deep meditation, even more if it's transcendental meditation, to calm down the stormy waters. You can find moments of mind fulfilment when you work with your intellect, by reading and learning and listening to whom you might consider a master.

But when I see people laughing hysterically, even if not high on drugs or under the effect of alcohol, I find them living an uncontrolled moment, a moment of madness in which you lose control of your own mind: the opposite of peace of mind or mind's fulfilment.

If you're sad, I can understand this because it is often related with loss: mostly self-loss. When you break a relationship you might experience loss, including self-loss, because you had balance while sharing feelings with others. Love is sharing feelings, right?

I mean, good feelings. So hate must is sharing bad feelings with each other.

Humans are so complicated in that way. Emotions only weakens one's mind, it seems that they only exist to confuse you and to give you emotional hiccups. Someone once asked me if being autistic would make me not know what love is. Autistic people do usually have a more logical mind, and I believe that we're not that emotional, but never forget that autism is a wide spectrum so you might find a bit of everything.

I realized then what I thought love was: not more than a projection of someone's love onto me. In fact I'm not sure if I ever felt love for someone, what I felt was the other's love projected onto me. Like a mirror which can also absorb the emotion. Like a second hand emotion. But whenever I felt love, it made me confused, like if it was blurring my mind. Whenever I felt hate from someone I know it's not pleasant because the vibration can be hurtful. Hate is quite grey, like dark lead. Sadness is more related with silver though. It's a cold light grey. In fact I relate human feelings with metals more than with colours, or with metallic colours to be more accurate. Gold seems to be warmer than silver though. Silver is cold. Peace of mind is not an emotion, so maybe it's why I relate it more with crystal quartz, and not with metals. The mind is definitely more related with crystals, and you can easily visualize the brain as crystals, from scales of purple, white, yellow, green… transparent crystal colours. Emotions and feelings (aren't they the same?) to metals. When I hug someone I feel the metal, if I really feel a good connection while hugging someone my whole body turns into gold. If by hugging I feel sadness I would see silver, or the dark lead of hate.

Curious enough when I need to understand "the state" of someone I would hug or simply smell their neck to understand how that person is. And whenever I feel the scent of iron, something is not well. The scent of iron in someone's neck pushes me back. It's often related with some illness sourced by the soul. It's not a pleasant energy or vibration. It means that the person is physically ill due to their own mind/ consciousness vibration. And you know that when someone's energetic meridian is too damaged that can lead to physical illness.

Being autistic I realized that whenever I go for a retreat, and would spend a year not in touch with anyone, I feel fulfilled, and if no one contacts me, I don't feel any external energies, just mine in oneness with the Universe, not with anyone in specific. The Universe is not tormented - as most humans are -, so the vibrations I feel from it are quite good and deep. And this makes me not only think that I prefer my solitude so I can be one with the Universe, but also that I don't want to come back to the effort of being social, wasting this tremendous amount of energy just by having a conversation with someone. My nature is not of a speaker, even though I taught myself to manage it well, it always makes me quite tired. In fact, it is not the speaking that makes me fully tired, but the energy I need to understand others and often people say things that are not that coherent with their own thoughts: and being empathic we listen to both and it gets very confusing.

But back to the emotions: do autistics really feel emotions which are not logical, or do we only think we feel them because we misunderstand and what we really feel is the projections of others because we're so empathic?
Empathy is a superior level, and I believe – tremendously - that we do not have human feelings because we are logical minds, and that is what leads us to not wanting to keep a conversation or not being social. Instead, we do have a tremendous empathy towards others, which allows us to be such empathizers with humanity and human related issues. I guess that it's due to that that we're most often just towards humanity, getting unbalanced towards human injustice. We might not feel love by ourselves, but our empathy toward others is so strong that we feel the other's emotions. And we try to make them logical, which can be quite frustrating.
I do not love, as I do not hate: instead I feel empathy, which can lead to compassion. I do not feel happy or sad, but I do empathize with your own feelings. Even when I don't find them logical.

But then, the lack of knowledge of the mind that exists in the west, plus the Collective Consciousness, will tell you differently. Think about Christmas for example: even if you don't go out of your home the whole month of December, not connecting with TV or internet, you will still feel the collective energy. I'm an agnostic by nature - as any reasonable logical scientific mind would be. But I do feel and incredible peace of mind during the morning of Christmas day. There's a relaxing and silent energy "in the air". But before that night, people are stressed from shopping, and marketing is geared towards family and shopping. And this is not that subliminal anymore. This is why the rate of suicide increases: people feel much more loneliness due to the family marketing. And here do not mistake solitude (the chosen path of self fulfilment) with loneliness (the imposed one or self loss). There's this collective energy, intelligence and awareness that we can't avoid, mostly because it comes with power and you have your channels open for the collective. It reaches you through empathy, thus through your subconscious.

I believe then that autistic people can be highly influenced by collective energy, as we're more sensitive and empathic. And most of us are not that aware of that, or goes through all childhood and learning process dealing with others, feeling the stress and emotions of others thinking that they're theirs.

Most meltdowns are due to others. Most breakdowns, most "anger" moments, loneliness, etc. are due to others. We don't know how to deal with that because they're not natural to us. If they were, we would understand them. We would make them logical. But they're not natural to us. Follow my thoughts: I find peace in my own silence, it's my nature. But some people wouldn't understand that. Some people need noise and a stressful environment to be louder than their own minds, so when dealing with autistic's peace of mind they get incredibly stressed thinking that we are wrong and unfeeling: and they project their own stress, anguish, anxiety, etc onto us. If you're not protected against those feelings, since we're so empathic, we feel them, they make no sense, and they unbalance us: then we have meltdowns. Our meltdowns and shutdowns, are mostly produced by others who are not autistic. The so called "normals".

If an autistic person is raised in a loving, peaceful, trustful and mindful environment, they will be incredible people. As opposed to an autistic child who's raised in the midst of a family that is stressed and lost and confused: a family that does not understand that they're projecting their own fears, anxieties and anguish onto the autistic child.

A peaceful, silent and mindful environment is the only way for us to develop awareness fully. And I want to believe that soon people will be aware of that and instead of influencing autistic children with their anxieties and unbalanced emotions due to illogical reasons of the mind, they will be influenced by the peace, silent and mindful autistic brains instead. If you're raising an autistic child, if you're a parent or tutor of anyone autistic do this experience: sit down next to them and experiment peace of mind, do meditation, find your own silence. Allow yourself to understand and feel our own silence rather than projecting your anxieties onto us.

I believe that the main issues that autistic people experience are essentially due to the collective energy of neuro-typical people: the stress, anxiety, anguish of other people's lives. If you're a parent or tutor of an autistic person: leave all your stress outside the home. Find your own peace next to the autistic one. Try to feel them and listen to their empathy rather than imposing yours. And stop judging, we don't do that either. We accept you at a higher level.

Or even better: leave the understanding and logical thinking to us when you're around: just allow yourself to feel silence and peace of mind. Our own. And when you find that peace you will feel empathy, connection and fulfilment. Don't try to cure us: we are the cure. Maybe it's time for you to understand that. We are cosmic souls. We vibrate. We are empathic. We have an amazing frequency.

You just have to tune into it and find the right signal. With patience and love.

You read it well: we are not the ones who need to be healed: you are. It's the science of the mind that we possess. Even if you feel superior because the collective society makes you believe so. You're not. You do have a lot to learn from us. Even if it's just because differentness is one of the most wonderful things in life. Normality is boring. Trust me.

It was about time to go to the dentist. It doesn't bother me because it's for my own good. Toothache can be quite uncomfortable whenever you sit down to have a meal, and recently I broke a tooth, which led me to eat on the other side, which resulted in an alarm of a cavity I didn't know that I had. It was time to go and check it all. It's important to have a healthy mouth, there's no doubt about it. As I arrived and the dentist fixed my broken tooth and scheduled a new appointment to fix the other: "we must kill it before fixing it" he said. "Ok, as long as you don't use anaesthesia", I answered. He looked at me scared, and promptly said that is quite painful and that he had never done it without anaesthesia; that I should reconsider. I'm sure I don't need it: I can easily go through those seconds of pain. I will not feel it. And if you use anaesthesia my mouth will be numb for couple hours.

The moment came and he asked once more if he could give me anaesthesia, to which I said "no, don't worry, just kill it". Just do your job and I'll do mine. I just need one minute to give instructions to my mind to not accept pain, or to embrace it in case there's pain. I explained to him that I had lived in Tibet and that I do meditation since I was 13 years old. He then gave me one minute or two, while preparing the tools.

I closed my eyes and immediately started going into trance, self-induced in a mix of self-hypnosis, transcendental meditation and visualization: I visualized my brain as if it was exposed in front of me.

I mentally left my body there: the body that could suffer with pain. I visualized the brain and its spots, or the way it was wired. It was, I must say, an amazing experience that I did for the first time: rewire my own brain in order to eliminate suffering and pain. And I was so overwhelmed and happy doing so, so out of the world playing with my own wired brain as if I was playing with the electric hardware of a huge computer with the shape of a brain, that it took me time to come back. I woke up from the trance when he said: "It's done". I asked him to say that when he was finished, because it would be the trigger I needed to come back to Earth. I didn't feel any pain, or anything at all. I was too busy playing with my brain, re-wiring it. Playing with its fuses and cables. It was a tremendous moment for me because I realised that it could be done.

How can you do this? It's easy if you practice visualization through transcendental meditation for example. Then, you only have to visualize your own brain with your own hands playing with the wires. Visualize the warm spots: think about pain and ask it to locate the spot. Now think about pleasure and ask it to locate the spot of pleasure. If you have any notion of electricity and how to wire a circuit it's more or less the same. Find the positive and negative, then disconnect the negative from the pain spot and connect to the positive of the pleasure spot.

Think about noise cancelling headphones: there's an external microphone that catches the sound and a speaker that will send back exactly the same frequency that will cancel the external sound giving you external silence. Re-wiring the brain is the same: find the pain and wire it with pleasure and you will find silence. But, as when you do hypnosis, inform your brain that when you hear a specific signal it must wake up. The signal was the dentist saying: "It's done". That moment the brain went back to normal and I woke up from my trance.

I didn't feel anything and I didn't need any anaesthesia.

There are different ways to avoid suffering, pain, or even heal someone: all through visualization and use of frequency. Here I'm describing a few real stories that I went through, healing others, or myself so you can have a better idea. Each moment, each healing has to be creative and take it by surprise. I rarely do the same. I listen to my intuition and follow it for a better result. One day I can heal my migraine using a turban to absorb it, other I can heal it with sound frequency, using a Tibetan bowl for example.

About halfway through a healing session with one of my patients who is a prestigious doctor, he brought me all the scans and ultrasounds for me to see, so it made my visualization quite easy. The next step was to petrify it and relocate it, or to relocate it and petrify it to be more accurate. I dragged the cancer to the kidneys and turned it into a stone. The next step was to chip away the stone without him feeling any pain, so I asked him to drink a mix of herbs at specific hours so I could connect and follow the trail and turn the liquid into energy until it made the stone disappear. In fact there's a Portuguese popular saying: "Water dripping day by day wears the hardest rock away." And that's what I did: using water as energy to wear the stone and make it disappear.

My healing process is usually through visualization transforming the actual source into energy, or frequency, to heal it afterwards.

Visualizing has always been a natural process for me since I was a child, but with time and especially my learning and practice in the Tibetan mountains made the use of it more accurate.

It's important to be aware of one's channels in this life, and if you are gifted with an open channel you should use it for the good of others, there's no doubt about it. Otherwise it wouldn't serve for anything, and the gift you carry will remain useless.

But I'm also aware that most healings and work in this field require time, learning, practice and especially energy and wisdom. There's a huge amount of energy spent helping others. To heal my friend, the doctor who had cancer, I couldn't do anything else for a couple weeks, because I was using all my energy to heal him.

To free my father from all his pain in the weeks before he died, it consumed me immensely and made me unable to do anything else in that time. This also must be changed: you must learn how to use the energy of nature and not yours: your energy is limited and you need it too.

How to do it then? Visualizing a triangle can be very useful: imagine the triangle with its 3 angles – 1 angle on you, another on the patient and the 3rd one on the source of energy. This will create the lines of visualization and energy: you visualize the patient and the source of energy, and then you create the healing energetic line between the patient and the source of energy. This way you're not using yourself as source, just as a channel, or as the controller of the situation: the healer. The source of energy can be a tree, the moon, or even the ground. You can also invoke the spirits of the animals, your totem, or any other cosmic source as they have unlimited healing power.

This leads to another question: which one should I call? My own spirit animal or the patient's? You can call both and explain to them what you need so they can work together, or in fact if it's easier for you, you can call the spirit animal of your patient. You can visualize it and ask him to help his connection. Most people are not connected with their spirit animal or cosmic entity, and we can easily do that. It's also a way to re-establish the connection between the person who lost it and their own spirit. I think that most people get ill after they lose their connection with their deepest being: bringing them back to their spirit animal or cosmic entity will heal them. And this way you don't have to lend your own spiritual animal to anyone else. Yours is your own.

The totem animal can change along your own life. Maybe in a certain period of your life you needed a spiritual one to guide you, and in any other phase, you need a deeper connection with another one, more physical for example. Or more intellectual/rational. They will show up for you when you need them, you just need to be aware and open to receive it the way it comes. I had a powerful one since I remember myself, who showed up several times to make it clear that he was there, however, when I came out of the 3 days of brain death that I induced myself, when I searched for it I realized that he was replaced by another, a much more powerful one than the former one. Even though I feel that the first one didn't abandon me: he's just resting by my side. I know that if I really need to, I can call him back and he will come.

The lost souls you heal can be very helpful as well. Whenever a lost soul comes and shows up to me – usually because they died with pending issues and they need to close their lives once they are dead – they end up being at my side for whenever I need them. It's not the first time I ask a specific one for help because I know he might have the skills and power to heal someone, but more commonly, I ask them to help and accompany someone who's freeing their soul, who died or is in the process of dying.

Let's make this clear then: when you need to heal someone physically or mentally you can and should call a healing source of energy, a spirit animal, a totem, etc. But whenever you're helping someone to die, it's better to call someone from there, who is already a cosmic entity.

As you can see all this is energy: you, the source of healing, the spirit animal, the cosmic entity, and the person who is in need of healing. We are all made of energy, of sound frequency. And the moment you're deeply aware of this, you're be able to heal yourself and others. We are all channels, energetic vibrations, or waves of frequency.

I'm sure Tesla or Planck could explain this better than me. But at the end this is just science of the mind, and you're the only one who can control your own.

Humans used to have compensations for their own differentness. A blind person often has a more developed sense of touch than anyone else with good sight. Compensations and defences, as we develop what we have, to compensate what we don't. I have a terrible memory for names, even more after the 3 days of brain death, but I often compensate with intuition. I remember how hard it was for me to read – and follow - a Russian novel with all those unpronounceable names for me. Most people though rely on their memory of names to show off that they know about any subject. In fact, most of the times they focus so much on the whole list of names they know that they ignore the main thing: the content. And I do the opposite: I naturally rely on the content, on the meaning, on my intuition, rather than the memorized names and labels.

When I came out from the brain death - and for some time -, I would meet people in the street who happily great me. I often got stuck, because I didn't have memory of them, even if they were once best friends. Immediately, and naturally, my first step was to identify their energy, and how it was connected with mine. In time and in concept, or meaning. I then realise the energetic compatibility between theirs and mine, and my feelings towards it. It has to be immediate and fast so they wouldn't notice it. Through the memory bank of emotions and archives of energy I would know my feelings, their energy… and finally their content. After that the name would come, in one of the multiple files I had of that person: identity, skills, friends, locations, hobbies, personality, attitude, etc. It can be quite tiring for the mind to not have immediate memory of names. But it is also an incredible mind exercise to practice. It keeps the mind awake the whole time as well. Awake and alert. Maybe that's why I often retreat far from people so I can have time to myself, to relax my mind from this and be able to use it for different exercises. To listen to it in its most pure form: intuition.

It is in the countryside far away from people where I can rely just on my intuition and connection with nature.

I don't waste that precious energy in searching for lost files with labels and names. I allow my mind to rest and follow intuition, nature, and concept. I practice visualization of energy and frequency. Also and most importantly, once I have this deep empathy and open channels towards collective intelligence, I don't have to deal with it. In urban areas, like in cities, I'm often interrupted by other people's thoughts and moods, as well as the hyper consciousness of the senses: smell, touch, sight, etc. I can be on my own without being interrupted.

This collective energy is quite interesting, and I often try to find the source of some moods.

We are in March now, and on this week there was a full moon in Virgo. I don't know much about astrology though, as there are too many names to memorise. But I always feel when we're about to have a full moon by intuition. And when we have new moon. But before the full moon happened it made it impossible for me to sleep for three days in a row. It also gave me some emotional unbalance and I found it weird. The full moon passed though, and the day after, talking with some friends I realised that they hadn't slept either, they had bad nights, and they had bad moods. I noticed also that the emails I got those days were mostly projecting personal frustrations, no matter if they were personal emails or business emails. People were venting their frustrations, not in the best mood. And surfing around the internet it was obvious that the posts and articles were weaker than usual, not having a good mood, no positive thinking. It seems that this full moon was, in conjunction and alignment with other planets, a nasty one that brought a collective energy of recycling the bad, a war between mind and heart, so people released and vented their own frustrations, emotions, traumas. Going through it is never easy, but in fact, - when you realise that people are venting and getting rid of their negative emotions - it's good. The day after the full moon passed, people were much more relaxed and happy and had good night's sleep. Maybe not many people noticed this, as they are not that observant of others. But the collective energy has indeed an incredible power over everyone.

If you're emotionally connected with someone, and that someone – no matter if they are at the other side of the world – has a bad moment, you might change your mood, if that someone is thinking of you. This is empathy: if I let something fall from my hands, I know that a specific person is thinking of me, so I send back a healing energy to that person to relax and everything goes back to normal.

I have a person that is dear to me who often projects other's issues so that I can rarely be with her both physically and mentally. She spends most of her time with other people and even if she says that she's not being affected by them, she projects onto others. Whenever I talk with her, either by phone or in real presence, I feel exactly what others have, the others who met her before or the others that she keeps in mind. I often feel sick when I meet her, and I'm able to tell what the other person is having or feeling. These projections are so strong, that is difficult for me to feel her own self. Her projections of others are stronger than herself. She has yet to learn how to not get emotionally connected to others, or to not be affected by others. This makes that being with her is often unpleasant, even though she herself is an amazing person.

Sometimes it's not the person's energy that we feel but someone else's that is emotional connected with them, so we must be aware and filter the energies.

One thing that is very important is to cancel our own energy, so we don't project it and thus be able to read the other's energy in a neutral field. If you work with a crystal pendulum you must have it neutral, not charged with your own energy so it can give you a real and actual reading of others. You can't project someone's energies to another person, you must disconnect or cancel your emotional ties, especially when you're healing someone or do readings. If you're emotionally tied to someone, you might project their energy onto your patient and get a mixed reading, rather than an accurate one.

The other very important action you should bear in mind is your own protection. And this is also related with the previous one: you should protect yourself with a shield of energy whenever you're healing, doing a reading or do anything related with energy and frequency. And this shield of energy you can easily achieve with meditation and visualization, which after some practice will become natural. As in self-hypnosis you can inform your mind that the energetic shield should be built by a click or a special word or command, and afterwards you can put the shield down with other word or command. Or just be connected with your own consciousness.

Being autistic makes me hyperconscious of senses, which leads me to an overwhelming awareness. Whenever I go to a hospital to visit someone I feel everyone's issues, so I have to create my shield of energy before going in. The same happens when I have to go into a hypermarket, or even walking in a big city street: to avoid overwhelming of the senses, no matter if they are smells, light, colours, or energies, I create my own energetic shield to protect me.

I often use noise cancelling headphones with music playing when I go out for a walk: this makes me feel more connected with myself and less with the environment. The energetic field, when you visualize it, can have the shape and colour you want: you might visualize yourself inside a blue bubble, like a soap bubble, or inside a white crystal pyramid. The shape doesn't matter, as long as you feel protected inside of it. Sometimes a bubble can make you feel better, some other times a pyramid can make you feel more energetic and protected. Follow your intuition and let it built the right shape and colour for you. Maybe if your aura is yellow in that moment, the natural shield may come in as compensation - the complementary colour: purple in this case. Don't impose a colour or a shape, just inform yourself that you need to build the energetic shield and it comes out naturally. Trust yourself, your consciousness, and let it go.

If you keep imposing you're just wasting energy, your own, and this will cause you to form a weaker shield, and you end up tired. Practice it alone, with meditation and visualization. Trust yourself and trust the cosmic answer to your needs. Ask the cosmic entities to help you on this journey, always showing a grateful attitude towards them. Whenever you're creating an energetic shield you're giving love to the cosmic entities, so they are grateful to you as well. It's a natural exchange.

Most of us are not aware of something tremendously important: that we all have traumas, and that most of these traumas are the responsible for our own fears. Fears that are so not conscious, that we're not aware of, so that we even deny them to ourselves. We often allow ourselves to be driven by inner fears without knowing it.

I lived all my life with a repulsive and sometimes aggressive response to bracelets, or even people holding or touching my wrists. Not that it often happened, and sometimes it was so natural that I didn't even think about it. One day I decided to make a regression in life through self-hypnosis, to find the moment in which I got a specific trauma. The day I realised it was a trauma, and that every trauma has a source that can be healed.

I went through several episodes in life in which I had my wrists touched, held, tied. But there it was, the first moment of my life on Earth: the moment of my own birth. When the bald English doctor took me out I was almost dead, I was born in comatose because my body rejected the blood I was given. The first moment of my life I was tied by the wrists and ankles, so they could keep me there without moving while they were making a full blood transfusion in order for me to survive. The first 3 weeks of my life I lived tied up, and I got 5 full blood transfusions until I decided that was enough and accepted the new blood so I could produce my own. That moment of awareness, of consciousness of the source of my trauma finally found a reason to "exist". So it's now overcome. No more trauma means no more fear to have my wrists touched, held or tied.

The moment you reach and understand the source of a trauma leads you to overcome it. To get rid of it. To lose the fears, even if they were just in your mind.

It's important for you to be aware of this: we all have fears, thus we all have traumas, even if you deny it. Most often you think it's a part of yourself and do not even think it's a trauma or a fear. You think it's just a part of your own personality. So you don't overcome the fear because you don't recognise it as such. And not being aware of them, you end up doing the same mistakes over and over. You don't go forward, not knowing why. You get stuck, and you're not even accepting it because you are not conscious of it. The mind does that: it creates filters, so you can have traumas and you're not aware of them.

In my experience, hypnosis, or even self-hypnosis, is the best way to be aware of them and heal the source. You can also go through transcendental meditation though.

I met a young man once who lived in absolute fear. Fear of going out, of meeting people, and of living. He spent 10 years having a psychologist come to his home, weekly, since he was 14 years old. He contacted me, and when we went further on in our conversations I realised that all his efforts were going in the wrong way, so unconsciously he had been cheating the psychologist – and himself - as their work had been always a mindful process. He never opened his consciousness to find the source. The moment I realised it I faced him with his own source of fear, the traumatic experience that he was not aware of. I made him face it first; and after his first shock of awareness, I healed him through hypnosis. From that moment he went out of the house without any problems: he healed himself the moment he was conscious of the source. The mind filtered the source, making him not aware of it. And all his work to overcome his fears were a loss of time, until he finally allowed himself to search in the archives of the consciousness.

The world of the consciousness is wonderful and you must be aware of that: you will be thrilled by what you will find there, and how you can heal yourself and others if you learn how to go deeper, without fears. But yes, it's important that you trust the person who's guiding you in that process. You should allow yourself to open your mind.

We all have fears. We all carry traumas, or even accumulate them through our experience of life. You get attached to them as if they were part of yourself. You can even suffer in silence not knowing about their existence. It happens to everyone. You often get stuck in the same problems, no matter if they are related to work, love, money or social life. And the only thing you have to do is to get rid of the source, the trauma that makes you get stuck. To find it and make it conscious so you can heal it. It's an inner process, and hypnosis is always self-hypnosis even when someone you trust guides it to you. I can guide you, but the main work is yours. I'm only a channel through which you can rely on to find your own self.

When I woke up from the 3 days of brain death I felt unbalanced, emotionally or intellectually unbalanced, because I didn't remember my past, so my first step was to get it back. I went deeply into that until I got it fixed with all my memories back, or at least, aware of the inner path that I would have to take every time I needed a specific memory. The process of fixing the memory, going daily to my archive, the memory bank we all have, made me comfortable to use it whenever I wanted to. It became a natural way of working. If I need to find a special memory I just have to focus and go for the folders. I reorganized the inner archives. It was a long process and not that I regretted that because I needed it so I could be aware of my past and roots and funded personality, but during that whole process I forgot to live in the present. I created series of photographs though in which I explored the whole process of rebirth, the "Oneness" series for example, in which I brought the knowledge and wisdom of the old shamans, to give my life back, power, skills, sight.

Now means not only the present moment in which we live, but is also a result of our past. Now is made also of borrowed moments from our past. Yet, is the future, which is made by borrowed moments of past and present. Now and Yet are the powerful moments, but they would be meaningless without the past. It seems obvious then, that to achieve a better Now and consequently a better Yet, we must heal our past. This is not only crucial: it is vital. It's all energy, and it's all ours. We do use energy from others to build our own, as others use our energy in the process to build their own, since we live in society and we deal with others. We influence others as others influence us. In the best and worst sense.

- Don't you hate that ex-lover? And that ex-friend?

You just shouldn't. You must heal that, and this can be worked on in a logical way: whenever you hate someone who was part of your life, you're hating your own self, because who you are now, was also due to their existence in your life.

Hating someone you once met, is always hating a part of yourself that grew up to be you now. The first step is, once more, to be conscious of the source that created your trauma, and the second, part of the healing, is to embrace it and turn the negative that is rotting in you into something positive which makes you grow and heal.

And this is much easier than you think. I know that you're thinking that is easier said than done, but trust me, with the right guide that you chose and who you trust, this is as easy as "drinking a glass of fresh water".

In western medicine, if you go to the doctor and complain about a stomach-ache, he would probably give you pills to calm the stomach down. In eastern medicine, they will follow the suffering until they find the source. Maybe the stomach is suffering not because of itself, but because you're stressed due to a loss for example. So instead of giving you pills for the stomach, making it even worse since it has to deal with chemicals, they will heal the source, they will make you aware of the source of the stress that is causing suffering. They will heal you, instead of just curing your stomach. And since everything is energy and thus related, the moment you find the source, you can easily heal it, and the energy changes, eradiating and spreading a new healing and relaxed frequency.

If you start practicing transcendental meditation you will see that you will soon be able to visualize all these energies, the energetic fields, yours and those of others. The energy that rules the world, the cosmic energy of which you are a part of. And this is very important, being aware that your energy makes part of a whole. You, as energetic body, are related to the cosmic one. We are one with the Universe. And this, you, the Universe is what makes the collective awareness, the collective energy, the collective consciousness. You don't have to wait for the aliens to occupy the Earth so you can be aware of that. Aliens must exist as energetic bodies as we do. In this energetic Multiverse.

We are just living an experience as humans, what we call life is just a small part of it, as physical energy: we are so much bigger that our own earthly existence.

I, as a human, cannot heal you, but as a healer or shaman, I can use my own energy linked to the Earth and the Heavens, my open channels to guide you on your own healing. The process of healing depends on you: a healer or a shaman can only guide you in your own process. It's always a self-healing process, as we are just open channels connecting the worlds. Connecting cosmic energies. The main element of our own existence.

And this is what this book is about: the moment you're able to visualize and understand that you're a body of energy; you'll take control of your own life. The concept of telepathy, healing through energy, or even teleportation will all make sense to you. And all this is being achieved by science, in due time. It's no longer a science fiction movie, and you don't even have to follow the Buddhist science of the mind. It's here. It's you. It's me. It's the whole Universe. All this has been a subject of study by scientists and physicians. Tesla, Einstein, Planck… It only requires deep knowledge of one's mind, the wonderful world of the consciousness through which we are all connected within the Universe.

The Cosmic Consciousness.

I became aware of this even since I was a child, but that was only awareness, and from there to acceptance is a long path. Not only the need to understand, but also the learning process so we can manage it. I'm still learning, every day, every moment I learn. In every practice, in every thing I do, no mater if walking along the shore or in deep transcendental meditation. We also need to overcome our fears, and in my case this was also a long process: the more I was aware of, the more I feared.

When you're just a child and someone dear to you says that they have skin cancer showing you a black spot on their skin, and you look at it saying: "no you have not" while your own consciousness just sees it as a spot of energy and throws it into the cosmos... and the next moment the real black spot no longer exist, and the next test shows nothing... it starts worrying you, because you realise the power of visualizing energy, the consciousness of energy itself and that we are nothing else but energy. I could write a book with just examples, and each one made me fear even more: the consciousness that you can heal, side by side with the consciousness that you can kill using the same tools and skills. You need to tame yourself to never feel hate, because hate can be quite powerful with incredible repercussions. The healer must first work on his own personality, and the most important thing is knowing that you yourself are not powerful: you just have open channels of energy that allows you to heal. You're just a body of energy like any other. And the more good you do, the more good will come back to you. It's a natural and universal law that you must be aware of. Finally, the healer should have no emotional attachments to the patient. An emotional attachment can be fatal to the patient.

When you have open channels that allows you to help lost souls who trust you, who come to you asking for help, you should use them and be useful. It must be terrible to die with pending issues, and if we can help free the lost souls who are still attached here, we're cleaning the Universe itself. The same happens when you heal someone who's suffering, no matter if it's physical or soul's pain, you're giving the Universe a better energy, recycling its own energy, using its own energy and frequency, giving a new sense of vibration around you.

I wrote before couple of stories on my dealing with lost souls who were still emotionally attached and what I did to free them. The examples I write in these books are nothing else than showing you that not only is it possible to heal using energy, but also to guide you through the process.

To be more aware of the science of the mind, the power we have, the visualization of energy, I myself have been the subject of my own research. I often challenge myself using my own consciousness and body of energy to go through this process. I wouldn't practice any of these healings on anyone before I understand myself what I'm doing and the possible consequences, if any. That is why I went through brain death and came back. That is why I often go in retreat to test myself. To work on my consciousness and on my body of energy. This way I know that I'm playing safe and wouldn't put anyone in danger. Your mind is the ultimate one who can decide your own path. I can heal you only if you allow me to. I will not heal you if you do not ask me. I shall do no practices on you unless I have your own permission and agreement. If you have someone who needs to free their soul, it's not you who should ask me to do so: it must be the one who needs their soul to be free.

In the case of my father it was him who asked me, so I took his pain away to make him feel more relaxed, we talked and only with his agreement I freed his own soul so it could depart from his body, conscious that he wouldn't leave any pending issues with him on his new energetic journey: the one without a body.

This is a practice that became a normal one to me, as several people asked me to do so. But whenever they ask me, the one who wants to free themselves, I always want to make sure that the person is ready to go, without pending issues, without emotional ties. Free to leave. A few times it has happened that after our healing process began they decided that they still have things to do here as physical beings. Then, I just heal them so they can have it easier.

One of the things that I struggled with through my life was "the visions". Not the regular visualizations, but the visions, no matter while awake or in a dream like state. It is not easy, unless induced, to understand if a vision is a flash back into the past, a subconscious worry or a premonition. Sometimes they are so coded or encrypted that we're only aware of their meaning when it's too late. Then we think: "ouch, I should have listened to my consciousness… instead of trying to rationalize it". That's the point. Whenever you try to rationalize you're blocking your intuition. And that can be a hard task since we grow up in a rational/logical society, which teaches us to think instead of to feel. To listen to our own consciousness. So whenever you have a vision, not knowing if it's a prediction or premonition, or a flash back, or even a dream – as in freeing your own worries -, just turn off the intellectual part and let your intuition guide you. The consciousness, the pure one is often right, much more than the logical thinking, as it is connected with the cosmic consciousness.

When a soul, in its unique body of energy approaches you, they know that you have open channels so you can feel them or even see their body shaped as energy. The only way you can deal with these types of encounters is to talk to them as if they're alive, like you. Say hello, greet them and ask how you can help them. Make sure that they feel welcome. If you show fear, they will leave to not bother you. If you show anger, they might project it back to you. They need love, your love, acceptance and awareness… otherwise they wouldn't have come to meet you. They come because they need help and found that you can do it. The reason they come to you is because they trust you, when they found your open energetic channel. They need you, they need the very best of you and they trust you, and this is what you have to keep in mind. Do not fear: be helpful. And you will get their friendship and loyalty in return.

Many times when I needed help, for me or for others, they showed up, the ones I had helped in the past, to help me. It's an exchange of energy, we do well and we get good in return. They will not harm you if you do not harm them out of your fear. If you can't help them at the moment, just ask them to come back later, or tell them that you can't help them and that it would be better to ask someone else for help. They will understand you. And you can talk to them as you talk with your friends, gently, with respect. Whenever you talk with love you will be understood. Do not fear. The only difference between them and us, is that we have a physical body to cover our body of energy. And they don't, they are only consciousness. They don't suffer bodily issues, but they can be suffering from what they should have left behind, their past as physical body, their mind, their emotional being. And this emotional energy can be taken into another life, another physical body.

If you believe in re-incarnation, you know that one can carry emotional issues from one life to another. Our consciousness is a bank of memories that exists shaped in energy. And this energy we often take to another life.

When a lost soul comes up, it means that they are still somehow stuck in their previous life, so they need our help to clear, to finish their pending issues, so can go to their next life without worries.

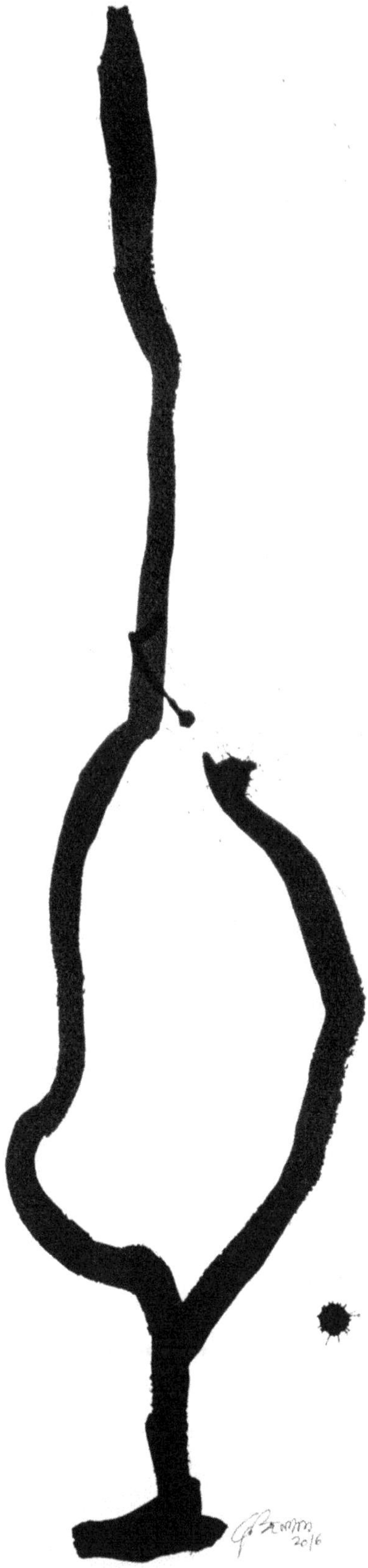
2016

All this you can achieve the moment you're finally aware of your own body of energy. Visualize through meditation the inner and the outer parts of yourself. Know how to stop though, it's important to have full knowledge of what you're doing so as not to get hurt. If you're really good in visualizing, you have to take full control of your emotions and mind. Imagine that you spent long time watching something blue, and that you kept blue in mind, and going through meditation you visualize your heart… and you impose your previous thoughts: blue. Then, you will visualize your heart blue and that's not very healthy.

So first of all, bear in mind few things that can be vital: Before healing, clear your own mind to not carry different issues, and be sure that you're in a peaceful state of mind, that you have no emotional ties and very important: protect yourself. Play safe from both sides, you're the only one who can do that. If someone comes for help, that means that they were not able to keep themselves clean and protected, so first of all, clean and protect yourself to be able to project the same energy and clean and protect the other. After that, find the source and heal the source. And don't ever try to heal anyone when you feel yourself emotionally unbalanced, much less heal someone with whom you have emotional ties because they can revert the healing. You must be fully aware of yourself, not only your skills but of your mind.

My whole life has been a learning process, fighting against fears, being aware of energies, of people's attitudes, of society. Society as a whole does not react well to differentness, and if you're different you must not let it interfere: for that you must tame your ego, the one that is not needed, the one that can be hurt. You must believe in yourself so you can overcome fears, but you can't allow the ego to interfere in this process. Ego belongs to you and must be tamed by you only. You are the only owner and carrier of your own mind, consciousness, and ego. You should tame them all for a better performance, no matter which one you chose. It's yours and you're aware that you can do well and be useful with it… or not. You can always cancel those skills as most people do, due to internal fears for example.

Learn and observe, observe and learn. Your aim should be wisdom, not only knowledge. For knowledge you might know all the names and labels and theories. For wisdom, you will know how to work with all that knowledge and skills. You heal not with knowledge but with wisdom. Connect yourself with the Universe and with all its elements. They are wise. Be humble as any disciple should be, listen to them: they are wiser than you.

Make sure you understand this: you're just a channel of energy carrying knowledge and wisdom.

Spend time feeling the rocks, the soil, the plants growing and blooming. See how they grow next to each other without problems because one of them is yellow and the other is red. One rose can co-exist next to a huge cactus. Both need chlorophyll to live. And most of the times they can even protect each other. They know that they're just energy. That they bloom as they die. Accept death as you accept life. It's all part of the same cycle of energy. The one in which we live. Death was never the opposite of life: it's just on the opposite side of birth.

In a financial crisis I'm often asked about money as well. For many years I struggled with being paid by my work because I always found money to be a dirty thing, in fact you can't even put money in your mouth. But money is also energy, and it should flow like anything else. We should flow as energy as well. We shall let it flow in order to live a healthy life. Money should flow too. Whenever you work you should allow others to pay you back. Money is the institutional energy that flows as payment. You can opt out by using another kind of energy payment though. But you must feel no shame or no disgust in being paid the way you decided to. It should be natural as flowing energy. I allow it to come to me, as I allow the energy flowing.

Think of energy, or vibration, of frequency. But don't get stuck in that. Don't allow it to be a source of anxiety, as you do not see helping or healing others as a source of anxiety. When other people need you they will come to you. Open your channels to give and to receive. Let others come to you for help and let others pay you back, with the same flowing of energy. Allow life to happen. Let go of all the anxiety and stress. Feel the energy that flows within you, from the ground to the Heavens, from the Heavens to the ground. One gives you air to breath; another gives you balance and a base for you to stand upon. They need you as you need them. Connect with the Universe: allow yourself to feel the connection.

I was focused working at my flat, which has several walls made of glass windows that I often kept open so the air could flow in and out. Suddenly I got a message on my computer screen: someone asking me to add him to a chat program that I left opened by distraction. I didn't know who that person was, but somehow I accepted and asked what he wanted after greeting him. He answered – not in a nice way though – that it was me who added him. In that moment I realised that I had a mission in his life, and I told him that. We then agreed to meet, but since I was in the middle of work I asked him to come to my house so we could talk, instead of me going out. He came within an hour. We sat down at the big 5 seats L shaped sofa in the middle of the open flat, each one in each corner.

Somehow neither of us felt comfortable with each other presence, but I had to lead the moment and make it flow. I started several conversations, but none of them was fruitful. We were on completely different waves. After an hour, he said it was silly to be there wasting our time and that he would go back home because his mother was waiting for him to have dinner. It was then that something clicked. His mother. Suddenly I felt a presence by my side, a strong energetic presence, I turned myself to the energy soul now standing by me and after greeting her I asked how could I help her. At the moment I didn't understand who she was, and I felt no shame in talking with her in his presence. She told me that she was his mother and that she was grateful for having opened my channels so she could finally talk to her son.

Damn, I thought: he just said that his mother was waiting for him to have dinner and now she's here, dead by my side. I had a click, a note that came from my intuition: the mother that is waiting for him is not his real biological mother; she's the one who adopted him. Ok, then, that made it easier for me. I turned to him and said that next to me there was a woman who said she was his mother and that she wanted to talk to him. He reacted very well though, but being logical he asked for proof that the person I saw was his real mother, explaining to me that yes, his biological mother had "abandoned" him and left him by an aunt to adopt him. He asked for proof and she asked what he wanted as proof and he replied he wanted her to appear as a bird.

That moment I released a silent "fuck" as I really don't like birds inside my home. They are meant to fly free, and I was not sure that I was prepared to see a bird there in the living room. She said ok, sure. And from the opened window from my bedroom a pigeon flew in, crossing the living room, going out through the opened window of my studio. Uff… the bird left as it came in. It was enough for him to be more certain. She then told me that she didn't abandon him, that she had a car accident with his father and it was not their fault they died when he was a kid, but most important was for him to know that they didn't abandon him to someone else. She wanted to make sure that he would understand that, because he would never be happy if he would keep thinking that he was abandoned by his real parents. I told him what she told me with all the details. He felt more confused than surprised. She then told him that she loves him, and that was very important for him to know. I kept being the "translator" or the medium in this process, or dialogue, or triangle. I needed him to make sure he had understood the whole message, and his mother was there to guide me. After the conversation was done, he stood up and left. His mother remained there though to tell me how grateful she was by freeing her from that pending issue, for helping him to release his anger, and that whenever I would need something, to call her.

She also told me that I should not contact him again, to close the deal the moment she would be gone. She left. I came back to the work I was doing at the computer and realised that his name was no longer there. Task done I thought. But then I looked back and there she was, to tell me that she wanted also to close the deal and that I should ask her anything, so I asked her to help someone who was battling with life and death and would need someone to ease the transition. She said to not worry and left. The person died moments later, in peace.

This episode of energy that happened to me few years ago shows the cycles well, and how we can all be helpful to each other and how we should let go. She paid me back by helping someone I needed to help. I helped her and her son.

But working with energy opens an entire Universe. Being energy, or being aware of our body of energy, we can not only be open channels to lost souls, but we can also heal through visualization of energy, help others through telepathy, sending the images their minds need or even in a higher level of being energy, to teleportation or levitation.

Even though all this made natural sense to me, when I arrived in the Himalayas and had to deal with all energetic sources, culture, minds, and overwhelming of the senses, I, most probably by defence, became rational trying to find a scientific explanation for everything that I was observing. For the first time I was having telepathic conversations in the most natural way. For the first time I saw someone levitating. For the first time I saw many things that I knew deeply were natural but never had the scientific explanation for them, as all we westerners need so much. I was in a trap created by my own inner battles between mind and consciousness, between logical and intuition. I even doubted the things that were actually happen, or the things that I was actually seeing. Then you have this oh-so-western thought: I can't tell anyone this or else they will think I'm nuts. But in fact we all happen to see different things. And we are all afraid to be different, thus not being accepted. But then, the moment you aim for wisdom and not only knowledge you get all the defences you need so you can go further on.

The monks started teasing me. They heard my mind screaming for meanings and science to explain everything. They laughed about my secret thoughts… and I ended up laughing with them.

They were right, I was being silly. I should just let go, and if something needed to be explained, the explanation will eventually come to you. As in everything: whenever you are really in need of something, if you're open to it, it will come to you.

After few weeks in the monastery's school of philosophy, in which there were around 200 Tibetan and Bhutanese monks and I, I was sent by the master to the mountains, to clear my mind, and to find silence, to get my main doubts answered. I left for the mountains. I trekked for several days, amazed with the new parameters of everything: colour, dimension, light, smells, touch… life itself. Crossing bamboo bridges and trekking over cliffs that I never thought I would be able to. I had no fear, I trusted myself, I didn't even think about that. I knew that nothing wrong would happen. I felt one and whole.

But we all have moments of uncertainty… and one of them came, at the wrong moment, so I fell. I fell down one of the cliffs and broke my leg. A fractured leg in the middle of nowhere without any way to get transport or phone or help or… was not in my plans. Even though I always carried a small first aid box with me, I was not prepared for a fractured leg. I was more prepared for superficial wounds or blisters. But no: a fractured leg, alone, probably 4.000 meters high, off of any path, stuck on a cliff, not being able to walk even less to climb up again. I got desperate but not anxious and this was what saved me: I allowed my consciousness take care of me and I didn't even think of letting fear to take control. I was on my own and could only count on myself. Without any interference of rational/logical mind, I looked again at the naked broken leg and immediately visualised it as energy, I went beyond the vision of a broken bone: I visualised the energy, the shape of it. The moment you visualise the energy in the shape of the broken bone it is halfway done: I "glued" it back to how it was before, its natural shape of good healthy bone. I was sitting down, looking at the leg, half in trance visualizing it as it should be: a healthy bone. I used all my energy to heal it not even being conscious of it. I don't even remember that I fell asleep afterwards, it might have been just a quick "nap" to restore the energies, which was easy since I couldn't be in a better place. I invoked the energy of the mountain, the monks, and the monasteries nearby. The prayer flags that exist all over the place, for the winds to carry the energy of the prayers. I became one with nature and allowed it to flow. When I woke up moments later, my leg was just bruised, and the bone was back to normal. I rested bit more, still confused from the whole fall, healing and nap, and went back to the "road". A couple of weeks later, already in town, I went to the hospital to make sure everything was ok. Reading the x-ray the doctor said yes, that I had a bone that was broken once, but now perfectly in shape again. But "once" maybe a few months ago, not a couple of weeks ago, as the bone was solidified already. I didn't dare to tell him what actually happened though.

I'm glad that I didn't let fear or anxiety or even consciousness enter my mind, or else I would have stayed there for who knows how long waiting for help. I allowed the intuition to work, along with faith, hope, trust and being one with the Universe.

Trust, hope, faith are not from logical minds. But we know we can have them. We always experience it at least once, and that gives us life. No matter if you have trust/hope/faith in one or 3 gods, in your own self or in the Universe.

Some years ago I lost them though, and only recently I realised that. It damaged me having lost it. Somehow I lost trust in others, thus I lost trust in myself. Or I somehow lost trust in myself, thus, I lost trust in others. I lost trust in the Universe. In me. Losing trust makes you also lose hope and faith. And with no trust and no hope you open a spiral of void. That year I had the motorbike accident, the eyes' surgery, etc. which ended with the coma, and brain death. I allowed myself to live, not conscious, without trust and hope. Without faith in the Universe. I turned off my connection with the Universe. I was living in Barcelona when this happened. Not conscious that I was being sucked into a void I allowed myself to fall, free fall. And I paid the price of it. I had to rebuild myself. But as always, there's always a good learning experience from our past actions, the moment we allow ourselves to learn from them, overcoming any possible emotional ties. In fact, only recently I understood the whole process, and that I lost the mastering of my own mind that led me to fall, to recover it and come back to life.

None of these were conscious, in both I allowed intuition to take guidance. Once again the intuition; that energetic part so much more connected with wisdom, with Universe itself.

There are in fact thousands of self-help books in the market, giving you tips for everything, by experts with lots of university PHDs. But if you don't have trust and hope, if you disconnect yourself from the Universe, no matter how many books you read or how many tips you follow, you'll not get your life back in the way you want.

You, by all means, must work with your trust (on yourself and on others), your hope (in the Universe) and be one with it. Be one with the Universe. Be one with yourself. Being grateful for your existence.

If you ever experienced losing someone, either because you broke a relationship or someone dear to you died, you know that you can feel damaged, lost, without hope, depressed. But the moment you reconnect with the Universe, the moment you reconnect with yourself, you become one again. You become even stronger than before.

Don't move.

Just close your eyes and watch yourself from above.

Visualize yourself as a breathing steady rock…
in the middle of a green field.

Now: allow yourself to feel good.

Feel connected and one with your higher self.

Δ

The experience I went through with the brain death episode, made me much stronger, even though I had to work on it afterwards, physically and psychologically, once I first went to find my lost connection, my connection with nature, the Universe itself. Mind you, I'm still learning, daily, with each one of the people I meet, with each moment of sun and each moment of rain. We are always in an uprising curve of learning. The moment you're no longer learning, you'll die. The Universe learns every moment: it's all about evolution. We adapt to animals and flowers as they adapt to us. Wild animals turn into pets by co-existing with humans, and we even lose body hair because we no longer need them. We have a clothing concept now as you know, even though it feels great when you're naked in the middle of nature. Yes, our skin thanks us whenever we allow our bodies to get some air and energy of nature without clothing. Being dressed is not our natural state. But we changed our bodies to accept clothing. Now the feeling is even better when we're out and naked with the breeze touching our skin. When you dive naked in the sea, the pleasure of the body swimming and being moulded by the waters.

Being aware of oneself is not enough, because it's not enough just having knowledge. It's vital to seek for wisdom, and it's vital to accept and embrace oneself as we are once we go through this path of evolution.

When you accept and embrace yourself, you're not only aware of yourself, but you're also sharing love. You will get rid of anxiety and depression, because they only come whenever you don't feel good and you're not certain about yourself. The moment you accept and embrace yourself, anxiety, uncertainty and fear will just leave. They have no space within your acceptance. They only exist to test you. And you can only answer with a "you don't belong in me". I am with nature. I am nature. I am one.

All this is science of the mind. It's when you're able to take control of it. In fact, you only experience freedom whenever you master your mind. I remember a monk in Tibet explaining this: if you want to experience freedom while you're sailing a boat you do not go to the front feeling the wind on your naked torso allowing the boat to go with the flow fighting alone against the waves... if you do this, the boat will sink and you will drown. You can only experience freedom when you have total control of the boat. Then, it's much easier to manage and sail against storms, having the knowledge and wisdom by your side. The same happens with the mind: for you to experience freedom, you must be in control of your own mind, and for that, you need knowledge and wisdom. With this, you will overcome any known or unknown fear, or anxieties.

You're the one in control. So you can experience freedom. Being one, you and your mind and the Universe.

It's not the mind that should control the consciousness; it's the consciousness that should control the mind. It's our consciousness that should guide you, even if you want to sit both at the table to argue, do not forget that most of the times, the intuition is the one who's right.

Give knowledge to the mind, and allow your consciousness to give you wisdom in return.

Take the mind as the library with all the archives and tools you might possibly need. Learn with it, use the given tools and you'll see that you don't need more than that; all the rest will come to you. Anxiety and fear blocks; whilst wisdom opens the channels of trust and of life. The ones that are so much needed that it becomes vital.
It is not an easy task to break the system, the society in which we grew up, based more on knowledge, not on wisdom. It requires will, to take action, and after this first step, the most difficult one, the doors start opening and you will find a new world. You must follow your intuition though, and relax your mind to the point of humbleness towards your consciousness. They should work together, as they complement each other. Consciousness needs mind, and mind is nothing without consciousness. Think about having a computer with just the Operative System, no other software. No apps to write or to edit photographs, no apps to chat or to listen to music. No software designed to

help you do graphics and equations. This is mind. Now imagine a bunch of software with which you can do all your tasks... without an operating system. It serves no one. You need both as they both complement each other. For you to go back to a document, you need the installed memory too. You need the knowledge of the OS to give you results as well. And you need the software so you can work with the OS using memory. This is you: OS, Software, and Memory. And to work with it you need all of them active and connected.

In this society we're only using one, thinking that we're using everything. We are not conscious of the whole, and when you live in ignorance you think you're fulfilled. You're not, there's a world beyond this superficial one. Even if the collective energy tells you the opposite. Sometimes I wonder if there's something in the water when I see all the people as if sleep walking, like sheep, without reacting. But I want to believe that people are in the process of awakening. It must happen, urgently, so there's awareness and real Collective Consciousness. This collective energy, awareness, and intelligence changes you and you're not even aware of that. You rely on others as a mental laziness act. Even if it's not consciously from you: it never is. When I healed my broken bone I was alone, in an environment of healing, of trust, of faith and hope. I could only rely on myself: I had to. If this had happened in the city, next to friends of family, they would have taken me to the hospital and it would have taken a month to heal. And I would have allowed it because I was being influenced by the collective energy. When we live in a city, that works on the base of mind and logical thinking and science, and we end up relying on it. Even worse: we doubt our own self, as we listen more easily to others than to our own consciousness and intuition. We even lose our self-esteem, faith, and trust. While we increase the collective energy by getting caught in the trap and allow ourselves to go with the flow. To be mentally lazy, because it's easier than fighting against it.

But this is a personal choice, and you should follow your own path. Your mind, your consciousness, your memory are yours, they're private, personal. You can have collective memory as well, but you should rely on yours and allow and work on your own consciousness and subconscious by yourself. To be complete and one. To wake up and be aware of yourself. If not, you'll die without even knowing who you were. Without accomplishing anything, the meaning of your life, as you spent it following others. You've been working all your life with just a small part of you. An important one, but not complete. You've been ignoring the consciousness, and the consciousness is the one on which you should rely on, the one you should trust and have faith in. It's not science as in

physics; it's science as in science of mind.
To be one, to be complete, one need to follow his own mind, his own energy, and only afterwards he shall send signals to the collective intelligence, not receiving them though. Then, we are part of the collective awareness, and we will receive from the collective or universal energy. Being a body of energy within the Universe, the consciousness should be the leader of mind and memory, but you're the ultimate leader of your own consciousness.

I exist; therefore I lead my own consciousness.

I will not talk about the existentialists whom I admire and respect. Those who have given me so much pleasure reading like Sartre, Heidegger or Nietzsche. The ones who denied that they were existentialists. But maybe we will get closer. Or maybe we should.
When you lead your own consciousness, which in turn leads your own mind, you will project it onto others. A sense of self-security and leadership as a statement. On the other hand, when you don't lead, you just follow it, you project insecurity and need of protection onto others. This is mind, not energy, since you can lead your own mind with positive or negative energy. But when you project leadership and positive energy onto others, you got it right. Nobody likes to feel negative energy projected by others, even though when someone projects insecurity you can

either turn to another direction or "adopt" them in a patronizing way.

There are then two different projections one can have: one from the body of mind, another from the body of energy. You can have an amazing fulfilling mind at the same time that you can have a terrible negative energy. And you must by all means work on this.

Negative energy will make you weak till you get bitter and rotten. And you will attract the same.

When you're healing someone, it's important that you wave your energy into a neutral state, even though projecting positivity. This requires practice and knowledge of the body of energy.

When you talk, or lecture, you should not only project positivity but also leadership, otherwise you'll not reach the targets. Or they will turn their backs on you. But then, you can project statements (which leads to no dialogue) or you can create dialogue, which makes you look more humble, and open to learn from the other side. Learning from others doesn't mean that you're insecure, that you will change your personality and certainties; in fact, they can increase the security of your own ideas. Then, when you make a statement it will come out bold, or irrefutable, because first you allowed yourself to understand all the other different points of view, you were not a narrow minded, you accepted others ideas so you can confront them, think about them without prejudice, and find the result of the equation by yourself. Only then you will talk as master, projecting statements. Even though I believe that a deep statement, even if very well evaluated, can change, but for that you shouldn't be proud and accept that you were wrong. This is not a difficult task to someone who's intelligent, who leads his own mind, but it can be incredibly hard for someone who does not, even if they think they do. An intelligent person, one who leads their consciousness, is always eager to learn and to change their opinion: and this is a statement. Every day we learn, every day we change; therefore every day is a day of evolution. Every single real intelligent person knows this, and has this as main line of survival, even if it's not conscious within. You are the only owner of your own mind, but your consciousness is the leader of your mind. There's no such thing as destiny: you are what you want to be, you're the only one who should lead yourself, your mind, your consciousness. But for that you must work on yourself not only creating defences towards the collective intelligence, but within yourself, working your own mind, leading it. What you cannot forget is that being a leader of your own mind, you must be clear, you must tame it, educate it, so it can inform and listen the consciousness. Logical thinking and intuition. Both are necessary and complementary. If there's a strong intuition, the consciousness must have a direct line to your mind so you can listen and accept it.

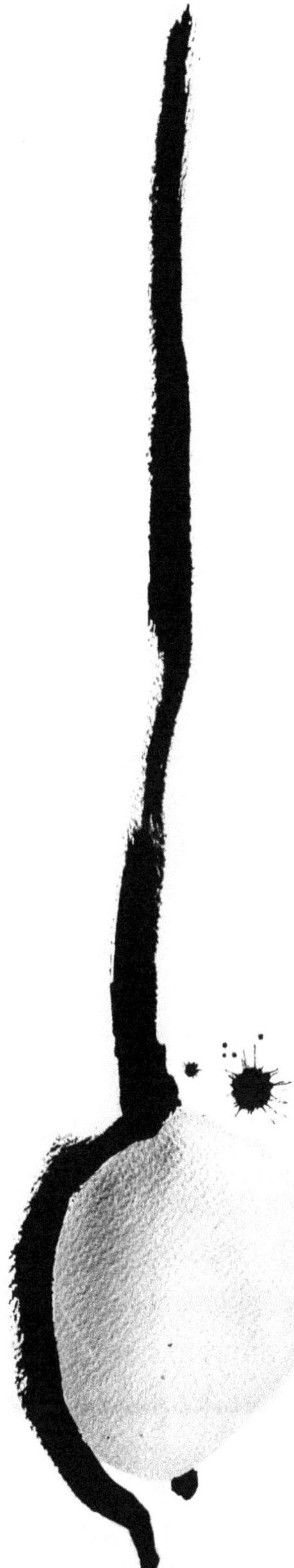

Both mind and consciousness must have the same weight and should be listened the same way by you.

When I was in coma, before going through brain death, I had absolutely no concept of body, of the physical body. I was observing directly two bodies of energy: mind and consciousness. One with a logical and rational speech, the other following intuition and reason. There was no place for emotion or physicality. What I was able to observe for the several hours of coma was my mind with two different energies, located in different places. The mind, an energy located within the brain; the consciousness, located out of the brain, as an aura.

I believe that our consciousness is indeed out of the body, of the mind, and it's where we have located our past knowledge (from our bank of memories, past lives, etc.).

Since then, something changed in me: I often see other people as "levitated" brains with their 2 energies, with their pineal gland as main engine… instead of actually seeing their physical bodies. Which is a much more interesting experience to be honest. If I always found difficult to label people by their race, colour, etc., now I find it almost impossible unless I really turn this visualization off and concentrate on the physical body. I see all kinds of brains though, but I'm unable to label them. They are in different colours due to their own energies and it has been a secondary study of mine, to catalogue brains by their colours of energy. Your brain colours though are almost never the same: most people have a colour for their mind/thoughts and another for their consciousness. This can also mislead you or the vision you have of yourself, not only the obvious misleading of others. The real colour must be the consciousness one, the one that should define you though. So then you struggle, because in the collective intelligence, the one to which is given more importance is the colour of the mind. The rational thinking. So you brighten it up to disguise the other: the so important consciousness, maybe because the collective intelligence tells you that the consciousness is your deepest sacred place, your most private book and sanctuary. Your own sacred book. The sacred book that is not supposed to be shared. So you develop an image, created by the mind under the protection of your consciousness, which, sorry to say: is leading you.

While the brains are hard (physical) the consciousness is soft (pure energy) as it is the mind itself, a product of these two. But, as any physical thing, brains are just a physical form of energy, thus, visible to common eyes.
The consciousness lives in a world of consciousness, beyond our own physical experience, in a transcendent collective experience, connected in a collective energy. And what you may call god, is just another consciousness that you admire and follow, but is not more than another

consciousness, one more consciousness in the collective Universe of consciousness, to which your own belongs as well. Your consciousness is then part of the collective consciousness, giving life to the world itself, which you can either follow or lead. You can either follow the collective intelligence, or lead your own.

This knowledge, with its acceptance and awareness, can give you power, or can give power to the mind you carry within the collective intelligence through the collective energy for a better collective awareness. It is a continuous act, constantly recycled as a living entity. It's not your heart that gives you life: it's your consciousness, your own energy. You project, and you get the new projection back. You're part of the collective awareness, and this must be enough to make you more responsible for your own thoughts and actions. To lead your own consciousness, which – under your command - will lead to your mind. It's all a matter of energy, of living energy within nature. We project and we get it back. You project onto your animals and plants and they project it back to you. You project onto your surrounding humankind, and it will project back to you. It's a world of consciousness, thus energy.

I exist; therefore I energy.

You are the only one responsible for your own consciousness; thus, you're the only one responsible for what is projected back to you. You exist, you project, and you get it back. You must be clear then about your own thoughts, and on the way you express them. They can, and most probably influence the surrounding consciousness, no matter if they are human, animal or plant. We are all beings of energy, producing, projecting and receiving from the collectiveness. The Cosmic Consciousness.

According to Richard Maurice Bucke, a Canadian Psychiatrist, there are three forms, or degrees of consciousness:
- Simple consciousness (which I call just consciousness), possessed by both animals and mankind;
- Self-consciousness (which I call mind), possessed by mankind, including thought, reason and creativity;
- Cosmic Consciousness, as a higher form of consciousness transcending the one possessed by ordinary man.

Cosmic Consciousness can be then related to Collective Consciousness, the global open iCloud of world's consciousness, in which each one of us contribute to. "A consciousness reservoir", as William James called it.
You can also find this same expression in essays by Einstein, or even in Teilhard de Chardin, a Jesuit philosopher and palaeontologist.

For you to have a better understanding of space-time being an illusion, think that your Now was the Now of a star sending light thousands of years ago. And that's why we still see its light, even though the star has died a long time ago. Reality is an illusion, like it is space-time. Or even time itself. My reality is not yours and never will be. My consciousness is based on my concept of reality and space-time, therefore, different from your own. We are beings of energy, generated by billions of years of evolution: life is an illusion created by our own consciousness based on our own reality and concept of space-time. The moment you realise this, the moment you deeply understand the real meaning of being energy, thus an illusion, you will be timeless and without a physical body. You will no longer weigh more than air. Being a body of energy is what can make you defy gravity, space and time. You will then be able to levitate, because there's no longer weight within you. Reality is an illusion just as time is.

This means that for other cosmic entities you're now either yet to be born or already dead. Even if you feel fully alive, for others, you're definitely not. And I mean, in this Now moment of time.

While the brain is physical, the mind is the action that goes through it. Mind is the ability of thinking, which has no physical form.

Consciousness is energy, it doesn't need a brain. So maybe we should just stop searching for life as we know it on other planets, but rather for consciousness. Within our planet as well.

You can then take the brain as a place in which there's a decoder to simplify your knowledge or awareness. Mind is the decoder of consciousness, which doesn't exist within the brain. Consciousness is a signal that the brain receives and that the mind decodes. They do have independent roles. Consciousness is probably the most pure and highest form of energy and frequency.

After going through brain death, I couldn't have a more clear certainty of this.

I was home alone that day when I induced myself into transcendental meditation to obtain the full bodiless experience. I disconnected with the world. I needed to challenge myself and empty my mind. But first let me explain the meaning of meditation. Mediation is not sitting down and thinking deeply about something. Meditation is meeting the silence, the emptiness within us. Being void and silent. Only after you achieve this, you can do focused meditation, after clearing your mind and finding silence you then can focus on a deep thought to discover its meaning. Transcendental meditation is travelling through frequency to free our energy of body, through visualization of energy to transcend ourselves.

That day I went into transcendental meditation. I often go into this state to heal, to fix, - others or myself -, visualizing our body as a body of frequency. When I heal someone most often I visualize their illness or source of pain as energy so I can calibrate and balance their frequency.

On the way to reach transcendental meditation I went through normal meditation and self-hypnosis, and somehow in this state, maybe to unconsciously find some rest, I called the health insurance company to send a doctor. I don't remember, but the doctor told me I did. It might have been for me to relax in case something went wrong. I somehow left the main door open as well. Again, I have no memory of this. I have no record of calling the doctor or of leaving the door open. I do remember the whole brain death. After going into this transcendental meditation trance in which I visualized my body as energy I ordered the heart to stop sending oxygen to the brain. I needed to "format it". I needed to clean it. I was in the lowest state of that descending spiralling year I went through. And this was decisive: I had to challenge myself: either live or die, but get out of the state in which my mind was confused and blurry. I needed to find the answer.

When the doctor arrived I was already in a coma, which soon resulted in brain death. At the time I had no record of the physical world anymore. I was just a body of energy, "playing around" with my own frequency, challenging and

recreating myself. I was brain dead for 3 days.
I did see my body, but I was not in it: I was just a voyeur of it. My body was levitating high above the void, relaxed. With a bodiless mind looking after it. Clear. I was just consciousness. Consciousness in the most pure form of energy and frequency. I was free of the physical body. As frequency I then realized the wonderful world of mind, and consciousness … and the battle begun. My mind informed my consciousness my aim and challenge and then relaxed. But then, as a formless being I had to decide what I really wanted. And I wanted to come back to life in a clearer state after 3 days. As if it was a deep retreat of my own being. I asked the spirits and souls that I had healed for protection and accompany me through this journey. I asked for guidance from the animals from the different realms and from the Cosmic Consciousness. Then I focused on my own frequency. I was relaxed, because I trusted the souls that were guiding me. I was in a deep state of consciousness. But the guidance from the Cosmic Consciousness gave me opposite information: I was told I was supposed to die versus I was told I was supposed to live. The inner battle between what we call mind and consciousness. After seemingly timeless period, a never-ending timeless state of mind, I followed this whole argument as voyeur of myself. My own life being scaled in values, although not being judged: just visualised. The reasons to die vs. the reasons to stay alive. My mission was

not accomplished as human being. This. It didn't matter what the mission was, what mattered was that the conclusion of my own mind was clear now: my "mission" on Earth was not accomplished yet, far from it. I had to come back, so I allowed myself to stay in this state of brain death for 3 days and informed the whole frequency that I was ok with it and glad to come back whenever would be the time, but no more than 3 days. I had to put a time concept on this: even though I had no concept of time I was connected with the Cosmic Consciousness. I kept observing myself as body surrounded by frequency and the clear image of consciousness as energy, external to the body itself, connected with the others. I was mindful as observer, a voyeur of my own body as energy surrounded and supported by consciousness. On one side I had the weight of the thought "die", on the other side I had the weight of the thought "live". Like a scale, or arguing with each other as in an ancient polis. Trying to give the other the most valid arguments, either to die or to come back to life. I was part of it myself, and only when they became too loud I realised that I was mind and it was me who should lead and make the final decision. I then informed the consciousness about my decision to relax for 3 days and come back to life. But I was out of my body, I had no concept of body, so they presented me with yet another challenge: "move your finger and you'll die, because you will lose your balance and fall down into the abyss" (mind) versus "move your finger and you'll fly to your own freedom so you can accomplish your earthly mission" (consciousness). I took the challenge and when I was finally ready to move my finger, informing the consciousness that I decided to come back to live, I realised that I had absolutely no concept of the body, therefore, no concept of a finger: how could I move my finger if I had no body? Another journey, the journey to come back to the body so I could move my finger? At the moment I knew that I just needed to inform, to make my own decision clear. I had to trust the highest form of frequency of consciousness. My mind was informed clearly: I allowed myself to rest bodiless for 3 days and then to come back to life. I wanted to live so I could accomplish my mission whatever it was. The moment I voiced the final decision, I allowed myself to rest. To move the finger so I could fly, no matter where the finger was. The finger was not important, the will to come back to it was: as a body of frequency. After 3 days of brain death I came back to life to move my finger. I opened my eyes to find it moving, as if flying, as a new born bird discovering its own wings. Wings that can use the wind itself to create even more wind. To open fields of energy, being connected, being one as a body of frequency. When I woke up I came back to the concept of body, but with a higher frequency, of body of energy.

I then kneeled and expressed my gratitude to the souls who helped me with this journey, to the ones I invoked and to the Cosmic Consciousness who also backed me up during this trip.

After this experience I took as sabbatical year to fix my memory and gain physical strength again. To be one with my body and my consciousness. I was mind. And through meditation and self-hypnosis I learned how and where to go to bring the memories back whenever I needed to. We are energy formed by frequency. Everything is there as it is, and you're the only one who can recreate yourself; the only one who can work on your own concept of being. Your space-time essence. Your past, your now, and your future, because all of them belong to the now moment.

Because I had a very clear concept of consciousness being out of our physical body, I also had a clear concept of space-time being one, being timeless, and being frequency. There is no now or past or future. Time exists in a triangle with equal sides and angles: one angle as past, another angle as future, another as now. They all depend on each other. They are all now and all past and all future. We are the ones who can lead and give to each other the top angle: the now. Some people will drag their past through all of their now and future, others will always neglect their past being only focused on the future, others can find the

balance and concept of all, living the now, giving meaning to their own lives. As a timeless consciousness.
Your life is then a triangle of time spiralling in its own space gravity.

While you were in low consciousness I have been on high consciousness. Low consciousness allows yourself to be driven by the Universe; high consciousness allows you to drive yourself, according or parallel to the Universe. You have to be aware of yourself and rise and increase your own vibration to a higher pitch, to take control of it. To have free will to raise your own frequency. I'm sure you have ever heard someone saying they were feeling low, and when you're low you're not who you really are. It's you who has the power to increase it, the only one who can be aware, tune yourself and increase your own frequency. Your own high frequency, thus consciousness.

We're supposed to learn because we're supposed to live and have challenges, that's why we're alive and here. Each one of us has one specific mission here, I believe that each one's mission is a self-challenge that we brought from a previous life, so we can learn. Some people give up, others can find the balance, frequency and connection to pursue their own mission, no matter which one they chose.

Your own consciousness was the one that created the mission you have now in life: the first step is to decode, to listen, to find the balance of your own frequency and to learn from it. We are just bodies of consciousness. No matter if you're brainless or have a high IQ. We all have our personal consciousness, which some call subconscious, while I prefer to call it just consciousness.

Consciousness is then where you keep your own personal and private data, where the whole bank of memories is. It's part of the consciousness, which *per se* is part of the Cosmic Consciousness. But it's your own consciousness that should lead the mind. Not the opposite as most people do. You're the only one who can lead it; you have the mind to decode your consciousness so you can take control of your own self. However, most people are taught to listen to their mind instead, and because others are influencing it, it makes you a plaything of your emotions and those of others.

You are the mind that can decode your consciousness, which is connected with the Cosmic Consciousness. And when you understand and absorb this concept of frequency you will be able to influence the Cosmic Consciousness. Lead yourself, master your mind to decode your own personal consciousness. You have all the information to do so. And if you're taught the opposite, you should erase that thought. Only you can and should lead your own mind, therefore, the personal consciousness of your own. Cosmic Consciousness is the highest mind-space-time Multiverse. What some people call god. If so, I am god, and so are you, the moment you allow yourself to be.

This week I stopped writing: I decided to listen to others instead of allowing my mind to flow into the form of words. I listened and read several lectures and essays by world renowned scientists, physicians, psychologists, sociologists and neuroscientists. From different ages, schools of thought and cultures. I was eager to learn and dig even deeper into this, but then something curious happened: I was not learning, I was opening the information I already had since I was a child. My deepest thoughts were the same as their final conclusions after years of scientific studies. They needed proof of all this because we live in a world in which we need proof of everything because we don't know how to listen to ourselves. Buddhism and other eastern philosophies have already known this for centuries. Scientists are now proving it to be certain. And the deeper they go, the more certain they are.
Your sense of trust, hope and faith should be aligned with your highest self. Your own essence. Your own consciousness.

Max Planck, the physicist who created the Quantum Theory, wrote: "I regard matter derivative from consciousness. We cannot get behind consciousness. Everything that we talk about, everything that we regard as existing, postulates consciousness."

The Universe is formed then by a great thought rather than by a greater machine, as Niels Bohr stated.

The Universe is ruled by this Cosmic Consciousness, formed by each one of our own projections of consciousness. This is the knowledge of the physical rulers of the world, the ones who also own the media, so they spread the message they want you to believe in, thus projecting their beliefs and thoughts to create a new Collective Consciousness. The day we unplug the media and connect with our own nature, we will then be able to change the course of the Cosmic Consciousness.

Einstein proved my own theory, giving voice to it: "The most beautiful and profound emotion we can experience is the sensation of the mystical. It is at the root of all true science. That deeply emotional conviction of the presence of a superior reasoning power, which is revealed in the incomprehensible Universe, is my idea of god."

God is then not more than Cosmic Consciousness, the greatest result and supreme thought of all the conscious projection of humanity and nature.

There is no greater machine, there's a greater thought: the

Cosmic Consciousness. Therefore, we're all responsible for it, we all give voice to this greatest thought, that you may call god.

While I was in the 3 days of brain death I experienced consciousness on a higher level, also as a voyeur, and a pupil of my own self. I became a disciple of my own consciousness. A pupil pursuing the path of becoming a master. I lived on the highest level of consciousness, in the ultimate state of peace. And of life itself.

Loneliness is the feeling of not being connected with oneself. Solitude, as opposite, is the feeling of being fulfilled by being connected with the highest consciousness of oneself. In solitude you will find yourself connected and balanced.
If you're experiencing loneliness, you should by all means practice meditation to re-connect to your inner self, to the highest consciousness, so you're able to re-create yourself and lead your own life.

Whilst you can control your 'self', thus your own consciousness, you can't control the Cosmic Consciousness or even global behaviour. Sorry to inform you about this. Although you can send information and be part of the Cosmic Consciousness spreading useful vibrations and frequencies, you can't be the leader of it.

You can be your own god though. You can master yourself then. You can control your own consciousness, and that is what you should focus on: your own mind, your own consciousness, your own frequency. Focus on what you can do, and leave the rest for the higher consciousness. Act independently so your consciousness achieves the higher state. If your goal is to master the Universe, you should first master yourself. It seems obvious. By mastering yourself you will then influence the highest consciousness and frequency: when you master your own energy, consciousness and frequency. It's all the same.
When you finally connect with your own consciousness, you're connecting yourself with the Cosmic Consciousness. You will find inner peace and balance. You will be able to be a body of frequency, thus be able to be part of a higher global cosmic frequency. You're now in contact with it, so you will get its response.

In my healing practices, when a patient comes to me complaining of pain or illness, I can locate it, but then, the most important thing is not to focus on it but rather on the person. On their own consciousness field of frequency. Whenever you feel pain, physical or psychological, after you locate it, you should focus on your own consciousness and frequency to balance your own vibrations. The physical body has an amazing sense of self-healing if you allow it to. The vibrations can go back to the right place if your consciousness is balanced and you're connected with your own self. You can reach it by visualizing your body of energy, your vibrational being, your sense of consciousness. We are much more powerful than you can imagine. And imagination is part of consciousness. You will not find the concept of time and space in it. Consciousness is the most powerful tool of the mind, so you must master the mind to be able to use it. You're a body of energy, of frequency, thus you can balance it the moment you're able to connect with your own essence.

When my father got ill, in the last day of his life I visualized him as body of energy so I could free him from suffering: so he could die at peace with himself. He gave up living, but he was in pain so he couldn't die at peace with himself. I visualised him as a body of frequency, released his pain, and he died in peace. I was prepared for him to lose his body, but I was not prepared to let him go in suffering. I invoked the cosmic entities, the souls I healed and the Cosmic Consciousness to guide him on his own journey. Free of pain and of suffering, so he could feel lighter to move on. My father now belongs to the higher level of consciousness. And it's up to him to come back and get another body with his own consciousness that he travelled with. We can only travel in space-time with our own consciousness, nothing else. You can't take your physical body, or your car or your house. These are just commodities that allow us to live more comfortably as physical bodies. When you die, it's just the body that dies; your consciousness remains part of the Cosmic Consciousness. You no longer need the commodities of physical life that we need whilst here: our house, food, cars, etc. We're free of all this when we finally meet our highest level of consciousness. But whilst here there's nothing wrong with achieving these physical goals to give ourselves a more comfortable physical life.

Live it, but master your mind so you can master your own consciousness, so you can be in a higher level of Cosmic Consciousness. Fulfil your own self and achieve your goals focusing on your own acts. You are what you think and pursue. You are your own acts.

Today is 20th March of 2015. The solar eclipse just happened. It's not the first eclipse that I witnessed though, but today I decided not to see it allowing me just to feel. At 8:30am I went into transcendental meditation. I am located by the ocean in a small town. At 9:05am something occurred: the moment of the total eclipse. I didn't see it, but there was this moment in which I suddenly and intensely felt the vibration and frequency of the Earth through my whole body. Shumann's resonance as it is scientifically called. The frequency of our brain is the same as the frequency of the Earth. When I was a child I felt this more often, in fact when I heard the frequency of the Earth for the first time I thought "this is the frequency of my own brain". It is the frequency of humans' brain. The Earth's frequency: 7.83Hz.

When I finished the transcendental meditation, in which you go into a void until you reach a body of energy, I came back to the computer to search for more scientific explanations about frequency and how humans' Consciousness is connected to Earth's frequency.

Checking a whole list of links and articles I found one quite interesting about a personal experience of someone who's paraplegic. Someone who has no sensitivity from his hips down: half of his body is asleep. In his report he says that when he listens to the Earth's frequency, he feels the vibration in his whole body; nothing else could give him feeling in his legs and feet. He says that listening to a record of the Earth's frequency he feels grounded, his own connection through a field of energy between Earth and the bottom of his feet. I found this quite intense: someone who has no sensitivity in his legs can feel them through the Cosmic Consciousness, the connection between Earth and a human's brain through the same vibration. I wonder if someone studied and tested this in a scientific way.

I felt this frequency intensely through my whole body, all this Cosmic Consciousness, all this connection between Earth and a human's brain. We do live in the same frequency, and this is what gives us life. Even if you don't feel it.

Cosmic Consciousness is life itself, this frequency that gives dynamic energy to Earth and humans.

This is what makes us a product of energy. And living on Earth we're nothing but energy, and our evolution is only due to it. Dynamic energy shared in the same frequency. Listening to a record of Earth's frequency I wondered for a moment if the planet's vibration is this because of humans' Cosmic Consciousness or human's one is on this frequency because of the Earth's Frequency. It's the same; they're related as everything else is. The sun has an apocalyptic frequency that spreads over the planets, giving live to all. Earth has this specific one, the same as humans' brains. And this, on its own is the origin of life, because it's life itself. Energy created by frequency. And this is what I've been using for a long time in transcendental meditation and healing practices: the frequency of the Earth, the frequency of the Collective, thus Cosmic Consciousness.

This Earth/Brain's frequency by itself is enough to understand telepathy, empathy, Cosmic Consciousness, teleportation or levitation.

Some years ago I was travelling through Europe with a friend, driving my car. I prefer to drive early in the morning but that evening I drove from one place to another that I wanted to visit. The gas tank though had to be filled and it was (literally) freezing outside. I was avoiding stopping, and feeling the freezing cold. I don't usually travel with other people, because I always prefer to travel by myself. And this friend was not that long time friend or even that close one. We were travelling together because he asked me to and I thought it might be nice. He didn't know me that well but we were in a good wave, travelling together sharing stories, experiences and silences. We understood each other and that was good. There was no reason to be judgemental towards each other. I guess that we both needed some time out, and were conscious of the each other's space. We didn't interfere with each other either. As if we were travelling alone together, with moments of sharing minds. I started getting worried about gas and a place to stay the night so I started to pay attention to any indication of a hotel on the road, village and specially a gas station. It is not snowing but the air outside is very dry and icy cold. I finally saw a gas station. I left the main road and went there parked at the gas pump. We were silent. I remember feeling panicky about the thought of me having to get out of the car and go to the station to pay for the gas and ask for a hotel. I stopped and turned off the engine. In front of me there was a huge glass window that made up the whole wall of the station with a few men inside drinking and talking, taking a break from their journeys. They were truck drivers needing a moment of relaxation, enjoying the heat inside of the station.

I got stuck. The only thing I could think of was how cold it was outside. That I had to go out and face the cold and find the door of the station that was not visible. I was living a controlled moment of panic. I was not seeing any door, only that huge glass wall with the men inside. I had to go out and freeze on the way in. I don't remember anything from the moment I decided to be there already to the moment I was actually in the station though. But the moment that I was consciously inside, I noticed the men were staring at me. I asked for a hotel and I paid for the gas. When that simple task was done I realised that I didn't know where the door was and asked for it as well. I don't remember anything else as if I was in a mindless state. I remember the men staring at me. Frozen. I remembered to sit back in the car after closing the door. I looked at my friend and said: done. That moment I realised that he was freaked out staring at me like the men inside. I didn't understand and asked him what happened. Why he was staring at me, and why the men inside had the same reaction. I was not conscious of what was happening. I was happy to be inside the car again and ready to move on. He remained in silence, confused, overwhelmed and the only thing he said was that he was not yet prepared to talk about what just happened. I insisted.

"You just went through the glass wall as if it didn't exist. You teleported yourself. You passed through it. While you were paying the car was filling up with gas. You didn't fill the gas tank. You didn't go around to go in through the door. Everything happened as if time didn't exist, as if you were not physical, a moment of flash. As if you went out and in at the same time. A flash. A photon of time. You're out and in almost at the same time while you're in the station and filling the tank. As if nothing happened. As if you came back in the car even before you went out of the car. As if you transported yourself through space and time to avoid the cold."

That explanation made sense to me as something normal or acceptable, even though I always search for a scientific explanation for everything. Time and space is certainly an illusion. And that was an impulsive moment of panic that I unconsciously wanted to avoid. And that happened. My mind tricked the space-time illusion.
By the time that he finished explaining all this, the windows of the car were covered by a layer of ice, so I asked him to go out and scrape it out with a card so we could see through it. He did, he needed that moment outside. We then went to the hotel where we spent the night, in the middle of nowhere.
He repeated a few times "I am not sure if I am prepared for this."

It was not my first time allowing this kind of flash tricking space-time though. On a scientific base it seems that these space-time trips can "easily" happen when you're either in brain death or in a moment of panic that turns off your brain for a flash of time.

The day I decided to do some needed work on my house I commissioned a builder to do it and I gave him the keys of the house. It was a small flat on the top floor near Lisbon: my very first house. The evening before the men would start working on it, I went to Madrid to stay there while they were working on my house because the men would be there making noise and I wouldn't be able to work. I didn't sleep very well all night though and fell asleep early in the morning. It was in this early morning sleep that I had a lucid dream in which I was sleeping in my own bedroom, in panic protecting myself using an energetic field. The mobile phone rang though, waking me up and on the other side the builder said: "Sir, the men are there in your house and they say that you're in bed sleeping so they ask if they can start the work, because you said you would not be there." I'm in Madrid, I answered. I'm in a hotel in Madrid, I'm not home, so yes, the men can start working. "Something weird is happening then sir, because the men are saying that you're in your bed. Do you have anyone there then?" In a moment of silence I understood. I was in panic and even though I was in Madrid I projected myself to my own bed, so the workers saw me and panicked. "Sir?

The men are freaking out because they say there's something weird there and they decided to leave your house and not do the work." I then explained to him that I didn't like the energy I was feeling of one of them and it gave me a bad feeling so I asked him if he could send someone else to do the work. That I was in Madrid, and not there. The builder then answered me: "Sir, I understand you more than you can imagine: you're too connected with your own space and you felt it being invaded by the energy of this man which is not good or compatible with yours. I will immediately replace them by 2 men of my trust. Don't worry and enjoy your trip."

This was what happened, and I understood it even better with his explanation. I had a moment of panic during my lucid dream. I was in fact energetically connected to my own flat so I travelled through space-time to be there, not allowing anyone to go in. But the moment the builder told me he understood, I trusted him and everything went back to normal. I pulled back my own projection; I brought myself back to me. And the work started.

This kind of tricking space-time always occurred in unconscious flashes or impulses, never consciously created by me. As the physicians explain, we can have these flashes of near death experiences in moments of panic or brain death. You can project your own body as in an out of body experience through lucid dreams, but more efficiently through transcendental meditation. These are experiences that happened to me since I was a child, even before I started practicing transcendental meditation.

It's easy to understand the moment you're fully aware that time is an illusion and we're all made of frequency, of Cosmic Consciousness. Then you can experiment with out of body projection for example. Or even shape shifting, like some shamans do. Levitation, as the body turns into energy, being energy lighter than air and thus not pulled by gravitation once it changes its own frequency. Telepathy happens when we're able to be on the exact same frequency with another, so our Cosmic Consciousness is aligned in its purest form.

Being autistic my thinking is logically oriented. I need to understand everything in a rational way. Since I was a child I had an immense curiosity for how everything works, no mater it's a telephone, a television, a plane or a ship. I first started being curious about everything mechanical, then about everything energetic. I had the need of understanding the mechanisms that could make things work. I was obsessed with Edison and Franklin and all these inventors and their creations. This by the time I was 8 to 12 years old perhaps. Maybe due to the fact that I started reading Jules Vernes at such a young age. I remember that when I was around 13 or 14 years old I created a huge panel as if I could drive a space ship through the Universe. It was a spare plywood panel from an old bed that was no longer needed. After spending a week creating the electric system, wiring bulbs and switches I sculpted my first staff in the shape of an Aztec Totem with almost 2 meters. I was ready to command my "space ship" then, and every night I "flew" it in my imagination before going to sleep and when waking up: I would travel through space and time in my sleep. I would sit down on my bed, holding the totemic staff on my left hand while connecting the lights as if it was a panel or the cockpit of a space ship. I have no idea where that "thing" is now though. But I think that my father was happy as not only I was learning while building, creating it, but also it was a way to keep all that electrical stuff organized. And recycled.

It was the summer that I commanded my own space ship. And I would see the Star Trek series using it. During my breaks I would be reading encyclopaedias for the youth, to learn how everything works.
Later on I kept needing a scientific explanation for everything that would occur. As if I needed a scientific explanation for everything I was feeling or experiencing. Even now I often struggle with the need to go beyond something natural to find a scientific explanation.

This week I took a break to do it. I took some time to watch amazing scientific debates, read amazing scientific books. To read Eisntein and Planck and Burde. As if I needed a validation of my experiences to understand them so I could write or share them in a more plausible way. Or to have scientific proof that what I experienced was real. I'm not sure if I learned anything though, even if I had an amazing time reading about them or listening to my thoughts that were debating about them in depth. It raised more questions than answers for me. But rather than learning, it gave me confidence to share some of the experiences that I went through, because now they had been explained by scientists and physicians. As if I needed permission from the scientific community to experience life connected by frequency. But in fact it relaxed me much more knowing that all my experiences were now being studied, and that there's a deeper connection between science and Buddhism's science of the mind. It all made sense as if it wouldn't have made sense before. They simply explained in a scientific way what I felt and experienced throughout my life. I relaxed. In fact my mind always relaxes when reading and listening to physicians and scientists. My brain relaxes when thinking deeply about what matters. It goes through moments of bliss.

This leads to another issue. In the West we're taught that we should rationalize everything. Being autistic this is something natural for us. Being a natural healer and since always having this connection to Earth, or being able to be energy, I am intuitive, and I often follow my consciousness. Intuition has never failed me… as long as I know how to put mind apart from consciousness. Some things do not need reason to exist; yet they do, and whenever you listen to your intuition rather than rational thinking, you might end up having a reason for it. But then there's a 3rd thing that you might want to get rid of: emotion. Emotion weakens and blurs your reason and intuition. Or let me rephrase: reason might blur your intuition, and emotion might blur your reason. So whenever you connect, visualise and especially whenever you're healing someone: never allow yourself to be emotional. Follow your intuition, forget reason and definitely erase any emotion. Emotion is too personal for you to handle when you're following your intuition. And the danger is when you blend all them: it often ends up as disastrous.

There's a reason why, if you're a doctor, you shouldn't take care of someone with whom you're emotional attached: emotion can take control, for the best and for the worst. You should learn how to control your emotional side, erasing it. Whenever you're healing someone, yourself, or just when you're following your own intuition. Never allow either emotion or reason to interfere with the intuitive process. You might need reason though, but only afterwards, not during the process. First listen to your intuition, and only then you might want to listen to reason. Do never let emotion take part in a healing process.

And in case you're autistic and have deep empathy, you can also feel this second hand emotion, when someone is projecting their emotions onto you and you feel them, but then, you must learn again how to avoid it, creating a shield or reflecting it back. It's important to listen to your intuition, it should trigger the consciousness in order to inform your mind, making it a main part of the logical process. But once again, never allow emotion to take any part in the process.

Even though I've always had a deep empathy with others, which allows me to feel others' physical or emotional pain, I don't "suffer" from emotions myself. I do feel, sometimes in an intense way, the emotions of others, whenever I allow myself to connect. No matter if it's love or anger, an emotion can influence a healing process, so we must remain emotionally neutral.

The same happens when you're using a pendulum to measure energies of someone or even a place. You must be sure that the relationship between the pendulum and you is neutral, pure. If not, the pendulum will be charged with your emotions and act in a different way. Before using it, test it. Test the pendulum to see if your emotions are not influencing the reading. You must always remain neutral no matter what. Let the intuition guide the process. If you

do this with a clear mind you will get best results.
When you're in the middle of a phone call you don't want the call to have external signals interfering or even disconnecting, you want the phone call to be clear. You can easily see emotions as an external interfering signal that will make the phone call unclear and with noise. Be intuitive, and only then you can ask your rational being for a clear answer. Be intuitive from the beginning to the end, without need of reason to interfere in the process.

Whenever you feel fear or whenever you're feeling anger, you are vulnerable. Animals perceive this easily. Fear and anger can damage any practice: they damage your pure energy, they drain it and you will project it. A clear and pure mind will help you, and you can practice it through meditation. Always be clear and pure in your thoughts and actions, only then can you be in connection with Earth's frequency. Only then can you be a good healer and shaman. Purify yourself and keep yourself clean, with clear thoughts. This practice is essential not only for you but also for others.

Whenever you feel anger or hate, you're losing and wasting your energy to the point of draining it and it doesn't give you any value, on the contrary, it makes you lost and weaker. In fact, you're sending your precious energy to the person or place that you hate. Love is a much more powerful one, and above all it's unlimited.

It's the most renewable source of energy that lets you surpass yourself. That empowers yourself. Always be grateful to this energy because it's this frequency that keeps you alive. While hate can drain you, love will always empower you. Don't ever forget this. Always charge yourself up by connection with nature.

If you have healing skills, you're working with frequency, so this goes both ways: you should always protect yourself from the patients' energy, because you should be always neutral towards them. If you allow emotions to accompany the healing energy and if you for any reason have any pending issues of your own, that you might not even be aware of, you will pass it on. And whenever a patient comes to you for help it's because they trust you. So you should respect that no matter who they are. Protect yourself towards them, because they probably don't know how to do that themselves, and never forget that the tools you have to heal can also kill.
Hate has the power to kill, as much as love has the power to bring to life. Always use your skills with wisdom, care and respect: remember that you're just a channel of energy.

As Earth gave to humans the same frequency that she has by giving birth to us, humans should give back the same clean and wise vibration. This reflects in the whole of humanity. This is the time for a special awakening, to the

collective energy, to the Cosmic Consciousness to be one with Earth. Remember then that the energy and frequency you produce is vital for the whole: Earth and Humanity. In the same length and wave.
There's an immense power in the Cosmic Consciousness. By now you should be aware of this because you're part of it.

Your own thoughts can change you as they can change your surroundings. We are made of the same energy. We need it to be alive. To give birth and to die without pending issues.
This seems like a new age speech, but there's nothing against new age if it's pure, even though there's still too many new agers with just willpower and knowledge yet lack of wisdom and skills. But this might be the first generation, the new generation is rising and they have a deeper and better understanding of this matter. Some people use to take magic and special skills as if they were living in a Hollywood movie. But with this new generation I hope that they will have a better understanding of it. There's also a rise of autistic people who are more connected to Earth than they are to other humans in social interaction because our brains are wired differently. And there must be a Cosmic Consciousness working on this. Do not make them feel the need to fit into society: they do fit in nature, we only have more difficulty fitting into a

society that is not connected with nature. Find your higher self. Find your connection with nature. Learn with nature. Be on the same frequency as Earth.

Knowing and being aware of this connection with nature made it possible for me to have a better understanding of humanity and of nature itself. By observing it. By listening to it. By finding the vibrational frequency of it whenever I'm in silence. For this, you must connect with your inner and higher self. You must connect with your inner silence, and never fear it. Silence brings wisdom in a higher level of consciousness.

Being a shaman is just that: being connected to our higher self, thus with the Cosmic Consciousness within nature. The one who has the skills to visualize the frequency so we can heal. To have compassion as part of nature. To be one with Earth. To live in the same frequency within the planet. The wise healer.

Mozart once said that he never asked anyone how to write symphonies, mainly because they came to him. The same happens here. I never asked how to reach the spirits or how to heal, I just allow the Universe to send them, open to receive and be directed by the Cosmic Consciousness. I'm open to be guided, and I manage the information that comes to me. I allow it to infuse me. They come and I answer acting accordingly. It's my desire to be able to heal others, and maybe that's why the cosmic world sends me spirits with unfinished business, with pending issues to come and manifest themselves so I can heal with movement, energy and frequency.

If you keep thinking about what is lacking or in what you don't want, you will attract it. However, if you believe that you can attain what you want and focus on exactly what you want you will attract it.
This sometimes ends up playing tricks, and that's why it is so important to be deeply connected with nature and not with ego. Ego can expect others' response, also creating anxiety, and when you're connecting with others with anxiety you will get their fears and consciousness. Whenever they're negative you will get that as well. Whenever you're connected with nature in oneness you act according to it, without anxiety, without expecting thus not being connected with others negativity. You are one with yourself and nature, only this way can you reach the wisdom to be aligned with cosmos. Only this way may you attain this dialogue with Cosmic Consciousness that you need to be aligned with the spirits and cosmic energy.

I don't look for it: my energetic channels are all open for it to come. And being one with nature I learn with it having it guiding me on this mission, with these tasks in nature.

A healer is someone who has open channels, who's connected to the high spirits. It's not an ego, it's an energetic body of Cosmic Consciousness, able to be in the same frequency and vibration as the Earth.

As intelligent beings we often need to have all our answers translated in mathematical equations, even if we don't have a single idea of what they mean. If I say that for me it makes sense that someone can levitate whenever he's able to visualize his own body as a field of energy, thus lighter than air, you would probably say "yeah sure…". But if a physician or scientist says the same thing and proves it with an incredible mathematic formula with 137.249 digits and abstractions you will look to it as if you understand automatically (which you most probably don't) and will take it as a warranty. We often underestimate ourselves, so we need others to give us that proof, that warranty. And if this comes as a scientific formula, it's even better. We forgot our own connection with nature. We no longer think for ourselves even though you like to think you do. Science is younger than shamanism. Shamanism feels nature and its energy and its wise spirits. Science tries to understand and make an equation of everything. We forgot to feel, to listen. We trust in science to give us answers, and we're happy to have them even though we don't understand.

Stop and listen instead. Be a pillar on Earth. Allow yourself to be energy, a channel between the Earth and the Heavens. Be energy. And you will not need scientific approval for your own thoughts.

I've been battling with this need for a long time, until I understood that I was losing too much energy by being updated by all this scientific stuff. Energy that I could use to heal instead: to be connected. I do read scientific essays and listen to physicians' lectures. I enjoy it immensely and they give me food for thought. It makes me feel joy when they finally discover the scientific proof for something that I have known since I was a child because it came naturally from within myself. I was born within the Cosmic Consciousness and so were you.

Maybe I just paid more attention to it, or since I was born in comatose I spent my first weeks of life in a near death experience, thus more vulnerable to these open channels, this connection. To this gratefulness that is life. But I do have a scientific mind too, and I embraced it some time ago. It doesn't interfere with my shamanic nature though. They embrace each other because they learned how to live respecting one another. Being autistic makes me a logical being, a rational mind. Being a shaman by nature makes me a more connected being, more aware of the spiritual world, of Earth, of energy.

Consciousness is infinite.

It's connected to Collective and Cosmic Consciousness.

It is out of our body, and it's the creator of it.

Ultimately consciousness is energy, frequency, and power.

At this point I need to go with a personal thought. I need to think out loud and I'm doing it here: each one of us is a work in progress. And that is the essence of life. If we had the ultimate truth, if we were perfect and finished products, there would be no sense in life. Being a work in progress is a great feeling, as we allow ourselves to fail in order to progress.

The brain death episode in my life was a wonderful way to remind me of that.

I probably had the worst year in my life when I was living in Barcelona, my last year there. Somehow, from one moment to another my life turned into a hell. In one year, due to an allergic reaction to cats, I had to go through an emergency for surgery in both eyes to not get blind. I lost my sight and took several months to rebuild the depth, volume, etc. When I got better, a flying "flyer" advertisement cut my eye, and I had to have laser surgery to fix it. I then had a motorbike accident on the high way that gave me a spinal disc hernia as well as other minor injuries. I was so incredibly stressed. And things got even worse because when you're stressed and negative everything starts failing and falling all over you. I started getting emotionally unbalanced and was not able to work. I was so stressed out that I couldn't create anymore. And the more stress I was accumulating the less creative work I could do. I did several paintings during that time only to destroy them afterwards. Some said it was my best work, but I couldn't even handle looking at them because they were the result of a lot of stress and reminded me of that period. I felt like I was going insane and I was not able to go any further. Unconsciously I got rid of all my friends, because I felt too ashamed of myself and didn't want them to see me suffering with frustration and stress. Even though I knew I was deeply loved, I hated that feeling of frustration and didn't want to project it to them either. I didn't even allow people to love me. I felt that I was not worth it. I started feeling weaker and weaker in every sense. I allowed the emotional unbalance to take control of me. I had the most incredible shutdown. If I was not even able to deal with myself I couldn't deal with others. I was happy though with the achievements of others. That was the only thing that would give me moments of joy: whenever I heard about someone who reached one more important goal in their lives. I was accomplishing nothing though, just digging my grave. Not even being conscious of that.

It was then that I decided to die and went into brain death.

When I came out from brain death I allowed myself to be helped by a good friend. I never allowed anyone to help me before that. I was probably too proud to accept help from others and I was the one who was always ready to help others in any way I could. One of the things brain death taught me was to be more humble in life, to learn and to accept. So I allowed myself to be helped and guided. First, I teased myself, putting that information into my subconscious, that by allowing myself to be helped by others I was giving others the same joy that I always got from helping others. I always took care of myself with anyone's help. I've always been the protector and older brother of my friends, young and old, family, and all those who were in my surroundings, just for the pleasure of helping them. How come I never allowed anyone to do that for me, when I always had such joy and fulfilment taking care of others? A matter of ego and pride. That ridiculous ego that is supposed to work for us, and that I allowed myself to become its slave.

This happens to too many people though: becoming slaves of their own creations.

I always loved to learn, to read and listen to others' points of view. I was never too fond of wasting my time with similar people: I always wanted to be surrounded by different people so I could learn from them. But in fact I did learn immensely when I lived with someone who was very similar to me: I grew up in fact, changing what I felt was wrong… in me.

Writing this book I wanted to make sure that what I was writing was making sense in order to be helpful and useful to others. For you. I never wanted to use this book as a way of imposing my own experience of life and my own ideas on others, knowing that they could be wrong. For this reason I decided that I would read and listen to different lectures: from scientists, physicians, philosophers, artists, shamans, healers, ordinary people, people that I admire, and people with whom I used to disagree. I wanted to listen to them all. I sometimes shouted rhetorical questions to study their reactions. I've been learning a lot doing the research and preparing this book. And this is the greatest thing. I'm not only learning but I'm also helping and being useful to others sharing my knowledge and thoughts. And if by being useful to others I can learn, the better it is.

Δ

After taking a break it took me 2 weeks to come back to writing this book, and since I have a terrible memory and did no previous planning or sketch of the book, I had to read it from the beginning. This book has been a stream of consciousness. I write what I'm thinking, or the thoughts as they come to me. This also means that not only do I write following the rhythm of my thoughts, but also, that I release my thoughts so I forget what I wrote. When I release, I let go, thus, I forget.

I realised today that I had a pending issue for the past 2 weeks, which made me become unfocused on most of my work and my life. I was not aware of that until yesterday night when the pending issue, or unfinished business, came to an end. I'm usually slow to get focused, but when I do I go deep and nothing around me can make me become unfocused. Unless I have duties, like cooking for all. One of my duties is cooking for others, which is another creative moment of the day. I enjoy cooking healthy and healing meals. When you cook with love and creativity you're giving your own energy to it. My energy becomes one with the meal, which will become one with the person who eats it. If you have to heal someone you can do it by preparing a meal or even a drink, visualising the energy of it and then visualising the person digesting it spreading the healing energy throughout their body, as a cleaner and healer.

Being a body of energy you can use it any way that makes you feel more comfortable, or the way your instincts leads you to use it. When you need to heal someone you just have to feel the energy: yours, the person who needs to be healed and the space in between both. That void that can be filled with healing energy. If I am energy, I can use my hands for example: by touching someone I can spread my heat, my healing energy. A hug can be a great channel of healing, that is why it is said that to keep yourself emotionally and physically healthy and balanced you just need to hug and be hugged 3 times per day.

If you're a healer and know how to use energies, you can do it any way you want. If you play an instrument, a sax for example, you can heal the listener by playing for them. Being energy is being aware that we're made of sound frequency, of vibration, of pure energy. By playing an instrument you're using your frequency to reach the other. And that can be in the opposite way as well. Right now, while writing this, I'm listening to the frequency of the Earth, the Shumann's resonance, at the same time that I'm listening to Duke Ellington playing. While listening to the Earth's frequency you feel more connected or one with the planet, thus with the Universe, and you can leave it to the subconscious and focus on any of the instruments played in Duke Ellington's band. I talked about sax, I'm focused on the sound frequency of it and I'm getting its own frequency to keep me healed. I visualized the source of energy in the sax so the frequency that it emits comes to me as healing energy: its sound waves. When you visualize the energy of an object you can make it a healer by itself. Don't stick to the objects-material, physical material, but visualise it as a body of pure energy. Imagine that you come to me for healing and I tell you to go sit on a pillow that is on the floor in the next room, which is empty, with just that pillow in the middle. I can visualise the pillow as body of energy, as a source of healing, so when you sit on it you're being healed. I just gave power to the pillow to be a healer itself, by visualizing it as body of healing energy, so whenever you sit there, you're being healed.

When you're able to visualise and be aware that you're just a pure body of energy, of frequency, you are in connection with the Universe, thus with its own frequency.

Remember that for you to have a lamp at home, many people worked for it. The designer, the electrician, the glass bulb worker, the metal worker, the person who packed and stored it, the seller, and the person who delivered it to you. All these people left their own energy in the object. And the object, in this case the lamp itself is connected to the cosmic energy by its own elements. You can easily have a lamp in your home as a source or healing energy, if you give power to it to be itself. In your mind you know that when you turn on the lamp in question, it will spread cosmic energy that will heal you. It's easier if you focus on an object that already exists instead of visualising one if you haven't acquire yet the skills to visualise.

Some time ago a middle-aged woman came to me asking for help. She was sick and feeling terrible, aware that it was affecting her deeply and that was a question of energy affecting her physical body. When she arrived I felt that she was somehow possessed by a terrible energy, carrying it and allowing it to fester within. She was going through terrible moments and not able to live normally. I asked her to sit in front of me and induced her into transcendental meditation. I lit 3 incense sticks from Tibet creating a triangle around us. I did a terrible mistake doing so: I should have located myself outside the triangle. I then visualised a flower blooming from the floor between us, as source of energy to heal her. But the moment that the flower bloomed and opened, it died. I understood that she needed more than just one flower, so I kept growing flowers and they kept dying. She was consuming so much energy to heal and to get rid of what was possessing her that I visualised a tree: and orange tree. The tree died too. Meanwhile I started becoming very tired and ill, blurred mind and possessed myself. She was using my own energy to heal herself, not being aware of it. Worse than that, she used me as source of healing. We finished the session a couple of hours later when she felt better. She went home and slept for 2 days to wake up happy, energetic and healed. When she left I felt very ill, my body temperature rose really high and I had fever (42C) while she was sleeping. The fever was not mine and somehow I didn't realise it: I was too ill to understand what happened. Then I vomited from the depth of my guts... and immediately I realised that she was healed. And me too. I was happy then as I not only healed her but I also learned that I should never heal someone without being protected myself.

You must by all means keep yourself protected while healing someone. It seems obvious, but I often forgot that when my focus was to heal the other. And for that you can use different approaches:

- Creating your own shield, or field of energy. You can chant a mantra and visualise your voice frequency going out, create a shield of energy around you, in the colour you prefer. If you feel connected with purple as protection, use it. If you feel that white would reflect more, go for it. Black is absorbing - if you go through chromo-therapy -, while white is reflective. But be careful, if you use white as reflective you might be reflecting the energy that the patient is releasing towards themselves again. Your shield is only to protect you. It shouldn't interfere with the patient. It should protect and remain neutral as you should too. So do not forget the main thing: keep yourself protected. Visualise yourself in a bubble of energy, or vibration, sound wave, frequency. I often use transparent blue, as a water frequency shield. Even for example when I have to go to a shopping centre or any other structure filled with different draining energies, I visualise myself in a bubble, a blue protective shield.

- Creating a shield around the patient. You can make it more physical locating candles and incense for example around them. If you use 3 candles creating a triangle, make sure that you don't point one of the angles towards yourself.

Take a deep breath now.
Close your eyes and focus on your breath.
Inspire.
Now let it go.

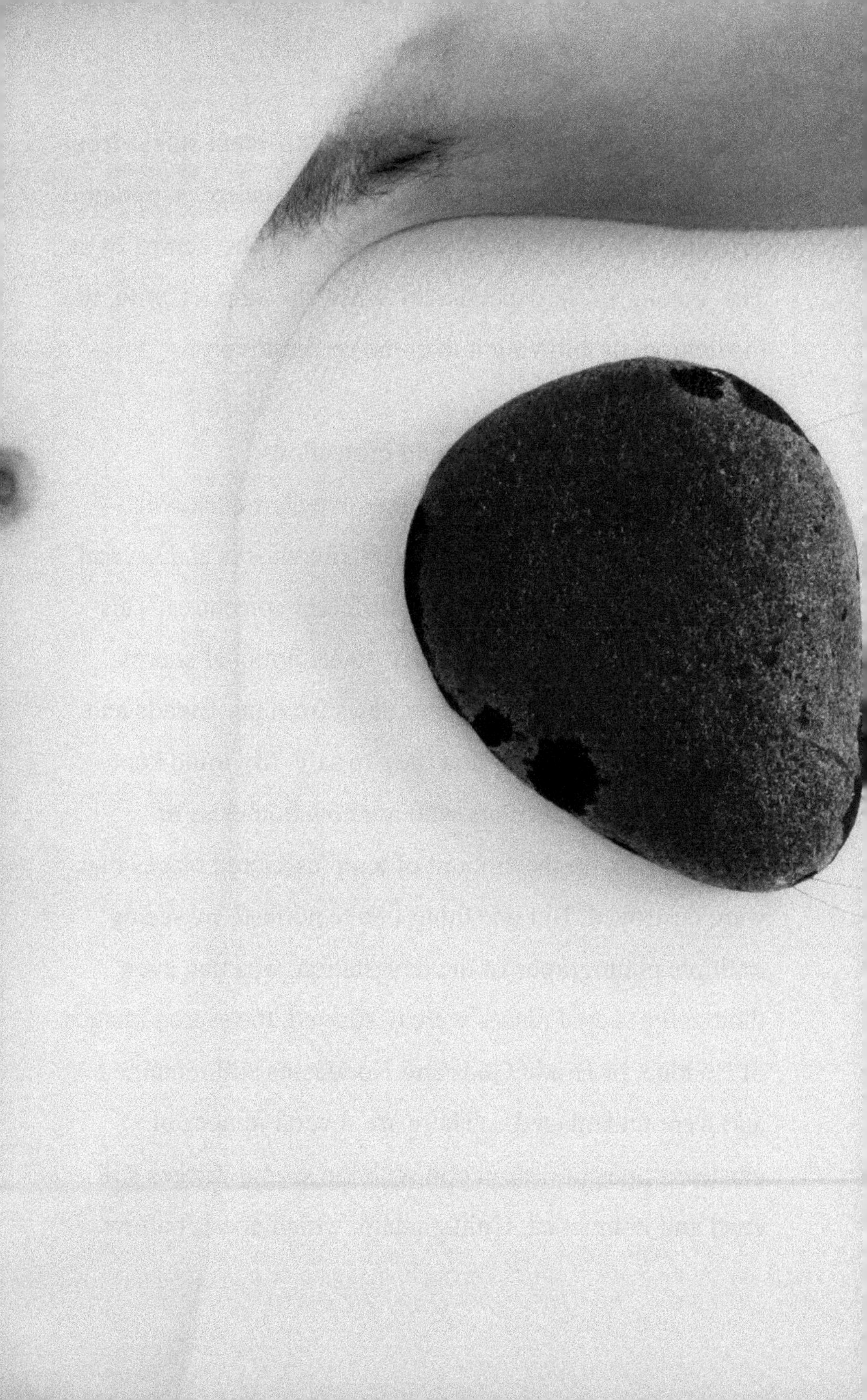

When I sit down in meditation I use a different shield from the one I use when I walk. I often visualize a pyramid structure, triangle based, with myself in the centre of it. The colour of it depends on what my aim is with the meditation, or allowing it to come up intuitively.

Sacred places used to be shield protections.
I'm writing in the week that a massive earthquake hit Nepal, followed by more than 100 aftershocks and several other smaller earthquakes with different epicentres. This made me be a bit agitated in my own emotional energy, even though I immediately got news from my friends and family there, and know that they're safe. My mind kept focusing on the survivors who are now homeless or injured. Also, on the amount of temples/sacred places that were destroyed. But one thing I have noticed, by seeing multiple photographs of the devastation, was that even though the sacred places were destroyed, the sacred images of Buddha, or Hindu Gods and Goddesses still remained and were undamaged... There are several images of clustered piles of destruction with the sacred images still erect and untouched. Unlike Islam, which doesn't allow

the worship of imagery, other religions and philosophies like Buddhism have their leaders, masters and divine ones represented to be worshipped, so the faithful people can find a presence, a soul in them, as a representation of the one. In them, the sacred images are blessed and target of all the prayers. People kneel or sit by them sending to them their best energies. Some of them have ancient sacred blessed texts within. In fact, recently, one important image was discovered having the embalmed mummy of a monk in meditation inside of it. They became powerful beings of energy, and as it seems, unbroken by natural calamities resisting time and space. People, sending their prayers to the images, are creating energetic shields around them. If there's an image of someone you worship, your energy goes to it, instead of going to the temple itself. The temple then goes down, yet the sacred image remains.

In the area of the monastic school where I studied and lived, most of the houses were destroyed. The temple remained: at the moment of the earthquake the Rinpoche was guiding a meditation for hundreds of monks. They remained silent while the Earth quaked. When you're praying or meditating you're creating a protective shield of energy, in a collective energy including all others. An empathic collective frequency is formed. The power of meditation, or the power of praying, is nothing else then a cosmic energy being created, one with nature, with Earth and Heavens.

I'm listening to the Earth frequency: the 7.83Hz sound waves. I often listen to it wearing headphones to be more focused on myself and connected to Earth. I'm writing outside, next to a palm tree, surrounded by green shrubs with an oak in front. I'm barefoot, as I like to be so I can release and recycle and feel the vibration of the ground. I mixed sounds playing different ones at the same time. Earth frequency and Tibetan bowls, or Earth frequency and Shamanic drums. Today I'm just listening to the Earth Resonance though. The one that was discovered by Shumann, that led afterwards to this major discovery that taught us what the old shamans already new and practiced: the Earth frequency is the same as our brain's frequency. The resonance that regulates humans and Earth. The same waves that carry the Collective Consciousness. And completely messed up now with electromagnetic radiations, mostly due to the massive use of mobile phones and Wi-Fi.

In fact, bees are showing us the real problem, as it is believed that they are highly sensitive to these magnetic fields. In some experiments trying to understand why there's a massive death rate of bees, they put a mobile phone inside beehives and the bees never returned there. They disappeared.

The only studies that were made to prove that mobile phones and other Wi-Fi's don't damage humans were sponsored by the major companies of Wi-Fi and mobile phones, so obviously they are not conclusive due to the collision of interests. Bees prove that by their disappearance and that can be catastrophic. That is why we always feel healthier when we're in the open countryside, far from Wi-Fi waves. We are beings of energy, thus, affected by micro waves that are used in Wi-Fi and mobile phones.

And don't tell me that you never felt an electric shock while touching someone else. It happens often to me when I'm more charged or energetic. More in tense.

One of the major experiments to prove this fact took place in a bunker, in which they put several healthy students and they deprive them of the Earth's resonance and they got ill, brain tired, vomiting and experienced dizziness. The moment they came out into the open air they re-established their connection with Earth and they came back to the normal healthy state. This experiment was done by the Planck institute to prove that when we're deprived of the Earth's resonance we become ill. And now our frequency is being highly interfered with microwaves, Wi-Fi's and mobile phones. We were born from Earth's frequency. We are on the same length as bodies of energy. We communicate with other elements through energy, through the same frequency of the Earth.

Research is showing that being exposed to this frequency is absolutely integral to us. It controls our mental and physical health, it synchronizes our circadian rhythms, and it aids our immune system and improves our sense of wellbeing.
Not only are we surrounded by natural frequencies; our bodies are filled with them too. Our cells communicate using electromagnetic frequencies. Our brain emits a

constant stream of frequencies and our DNA delivers instructions, using frequency waves. Without them we couldn't exist for more than a second.

This was proved when Montagnier discovered the connection and communication between DNA. A "detail" that defied the basic law of physics: all lives come from life itself. His experiment based on the principle that water has memory and can be a communicator of energy and frequency creating new life. He used what other physicians didn't: the Earth's resonance.

If you're electro-sensitive as I am, you might have experienced some wave frequencies whenever you travel. There's a highway that I use to drive through quite often, but one day a huge building that I saw being built started functioning, and since then, whenever I drive by it I feel an incredible spark of pain in my head, as if from the building a thin iron stick penetrated my brain. I didn't pay attention to it the first times, thinking it might have been a change of weather/pressure, a warning of migraine, or even a more sensitive day for underground water streams.

When it became the new normal, passing by the building, it was clear to me. The building is a hardware/software corporation receiving an incredible amount of electromagnetic waves, micro waves, with all the mobile phones and Wi-Fi's and wireless gear in there. Since they opened, whenever I cross that line I feel like my head is being penetrated by a sharp metal needle.

One of the things you should avoid so that your sleep is not interfered with is to have Wi-Fi laptops and mobile phones next to your bed. Don't even take them to your bedroom. Make sure that your bedroom is your safe and peaceful place where you can fully rest. The brain repairs itself during night-time, as the pineal gland produces melatonin, which is what we need to prevent cancer for example. If you keep exposing your brain to electromagnetic man made waves your melatonin - main anti-oxidant hormones - will be damaged and not be able to repair your brain, thus your own body. The cells of our body communicate with each other using light frequencies. Our DNA uses electromagnetic frequencies to reproduce itself. Whenever we're exposed to microwaves, mobile phones or Wi-Fi, we're damaging the natural resources that we have to regenerate and repair ourselves. This also seems to be one of the reasons for the increase of autism since we are beings of frequency, on the same wavelength of Earth itself.

I stopped. I was writing when I looked out of the window following the murmurs of the pouring rain over the palm tree. Then I stopped. I stared at the main big leaf that is facing me. How would be if I could transport myself and blend into that big leaf as a formless being of energy? Would I be able to discover a new world inside of the leaf and of the tree itself? I'm sure that within the tree there would be no boundaries so you can freely travel in the tree, just as their souls do. The fact that trees have their souls constantly travelling inside of them has always fascinated me. What would it be like to live in a chlorophylled world? How would be to be a tree? I stared, and I projected myself into it. I relaxed, smiled and allowed myself to feel good. This palm tree leaf looks like a peacock with its tail spread open. In green. Diving in a palm tree's open leaf, as formless being of energy. As one, in the same frequency of Earth itself. As a free travelling soul.

I never liked my grandmother very much, even though I admired her strength as she raised her children alone since my grandfather died when they were still children. But every day at 5 o'clock there was tea with cakes at her house. The door was always open for the family: no invitations. With 83 grandchildren, there was no need of an invitation: the table was always complete. People would arrive half an hour before teatime. I never did it though. I was called "Le Petit Prince" by the family. The dreamer who enjoyed being in silence in my corner drawing or reading. Or asking different questions from the normal. One day I had to kill some spare time though, and being next to her house I thought that I should go there, which would make my father happy. Her housekeeper opened the door and told me that grandmother was alone in the living room, and that she had to leave for some shopping. I came in and sat down next to her after kissing her hand. We had a weird exchange of words. Small talk. At 5, the old Comtoise clock strikes. Can you hear it? She stood up, a bit lost because no one came to tea for the very first time: only me. And me, I felt even more lost because I never felt comfortable with her. I stood up too. She then headed to the dining room and I followed her. Midway she asked: "Quelle heure est-il, mon petit prince?" I found the question a bit too silly since the clock answered just a little while ago – that was why she stood up -, so I didn't answer because I it's hard for me to follow up on silly questions. I didn't answer thinking how silly it would be of me to answer the obvious. That moment she fell on the floor losing her senses, like she was dead. I was 15 years old and I went there for tea. I looked to her and thought she was dead. I touched her and she didn't respond. I thought that this was the way people died. I called father then to inform him that she had died in front of me and while I waited for him to come I went to the dining room to have tea and cake: my actual purpose on the visit. While enjoying the tea I looked at her. She was dead: there was nothing I could do. So I observed death, trying to see a soul coming out of her body while enjoying the cake. It was my first time observing a dead person. My father arrived, and a few minutes later the ambulance. I interrupted my tea to open the door and went back to it. She was not dead after all: she had a stroke. When I finished the tea and cake, I left. They took her also. I heard that meanwhile she had some more strokes and became kind of like a vegetable. For 5 years she was a vegetable: never recognized anyone else or ever talked again. The 5 o'clock tea ritual moved to her bedroom, where now they would meet her around the bed. The bedroom was rearranged to be more like a living room where they would meet. After 5 years I decided to go there since my father asked me to, and I knew he was there. I went, and was informed that they were all in her bedroom. I came in, and kissed everyone who was there, uncles, aunts and cousins. My father then told me that I should go

[172]and kiss grandmother. I found this to be a very weird thing to do, because she looked like a dead person in bed, like if she was embalmed. I used to kiss her hand before, but now she wouldn't give me her hand for me to kiss.
I put my right hand over her left hand, and bending myself I kissed her forehead: "Bonjour ma grand'mère".
Awkward, because I felt like I was kissing an embalmed corpse, but I left my hand over hers, as if sending her some living heat. Some healing.
That moment she opened the eyes and asked: "Quelle heure est-il, mon petit prince?". I felt like I was hit by a bolt of lightning.
For her, the tea was the most important moment of the day, the moment in which she would be with her family. The only reason for her to be alive. When she had the first stroke, she was with me and I left her un-answered. She "died" with a pending issue. She was a strong woman, so she wouldn't allow herself to die before accomplishing her mission. And not answering her, I kept her in that state. These were my immediate thoughts, so I immediately answered her: "it's late, everybody left already and I have to go back home as well. You may rest in peace now".
She closed her eyes again and died with a restful expression on her face.

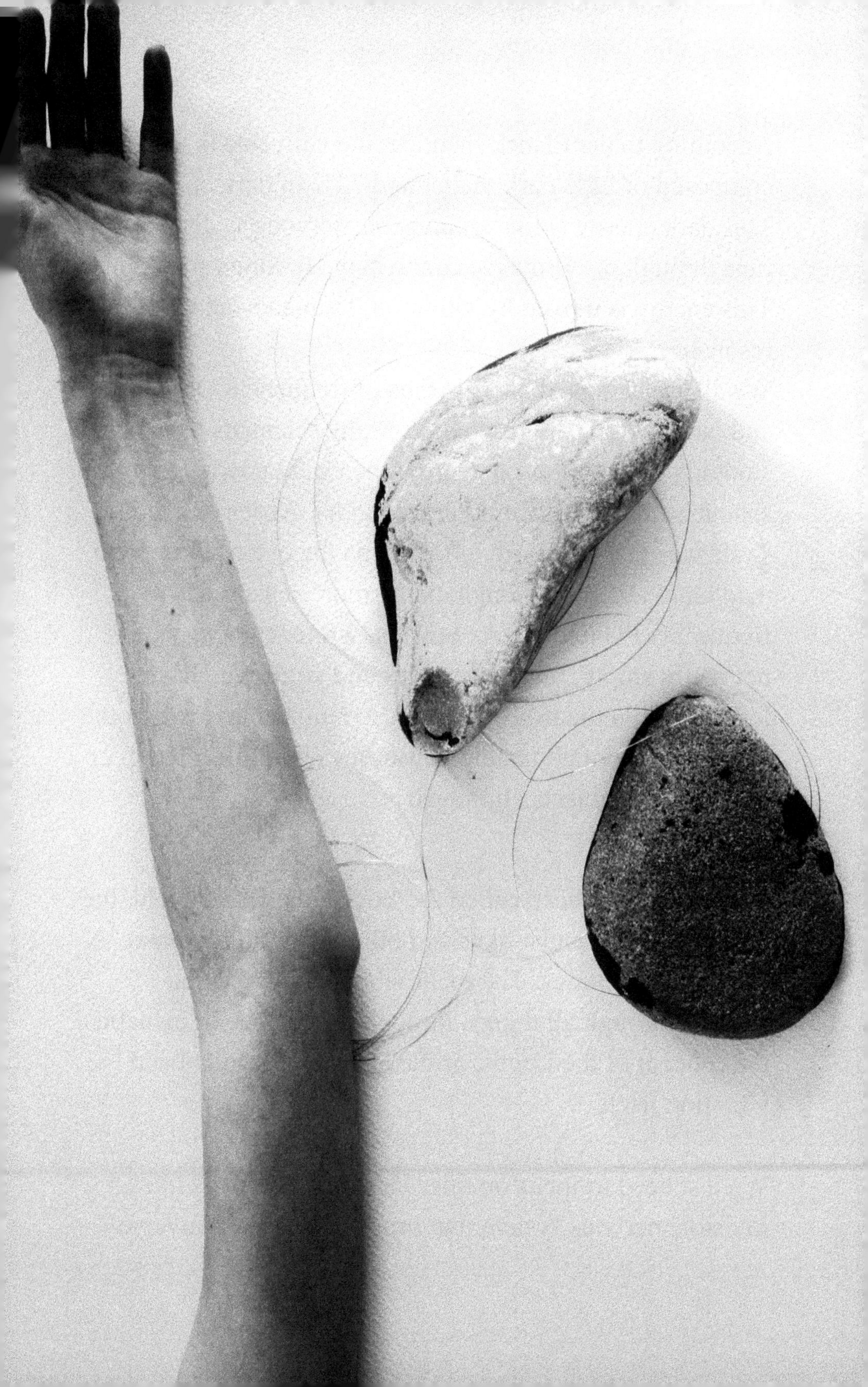

According to the Planck Institute, the Universe is composed of 23% dark matter and 73% of dark energy. This dark energy is like an invisible nervous system that runs through the Universe connecting all things and beings. This energy is moved by vibration, frequency and resonance.

We all are beings of energy, thus of frequency. Our inner and outer worlds are resonance. Many scientists have been studying old cultures on energy: their old knowledge from shamans and sages, from Peru, to India, Africa or Tibet. Tesla was just one more of them, maybe one of those who paid more attention though, being more sensitive to frequency. Planck too. As Einstein wrote, empty space is not really empty. Shamans, sages and yogis who have looked within themselves have also realized that within the emptiness is unfathomable power, a web of information or energy that connects all things.

This matrix has been called the Logos, the Higgs Field, the Primordial OM and a thousand other names throughout history and cultures. The main vibratory source that extends through all things, through the science of cymatics, the concept of the Logos, or the Universe as sound and vibration itself.

We just need to focus on this: This dark energy is like an invisible nervous system that runs through the Universe connecting all things and beings. This energy is moved by vibration, frequency and resonance. The greatest power. This primary substance, like tiny invisible particles, travels trillions of time per second. From one being to another through this Cosmic Consciousness. The exact moment I think about you, you will receive the message. This is our own reality: the whole Universe is made of energy and communicates through frequency. Like an invisible nervous system connecting us all.

If you practice real meditation, whenever your mind remains still, your consciousness is able to visualize the existence of this cosmic frequency. Consciousness is what drives the frequency that connects beings. Whenever you master your mind through meditation, you'll be able to work with the energies and frequencies, so you can heal others. So you can connect with beings and souls on a higher level.

If you cut yourself and it gets infected, it can be just because you sent that thought to the Universe, to which the Universe replied to you as a confirmation. As it always does. But if instead you think positive, look at the cut and think that the cut is nothing and it will close as fast as it opened, the cut will disappear. I barely have visible scars on my body: some disappear whilst some others just shrunk. It's harder though when something happens when you're with other people because we tend to rely on others. Also because we're humans, so we can feel emotional. Another factor is that sometimes if you're too empathic you can even feel others' pain, and if you don't know the other's energy well, you might even suffer from it as if the pain was yours.

This happens quite often, even if you're not aware of it. Yesterday for example when I came out of the shower I had a massive pain in my lower back without any apparent reason, right there by the kidneys. For some time after it was even difficult for me to move or walk. I sat down, turned the computer on, downloaded emails so I could forget the pain doing something more useful, or that I had to do. Among several emails I got was one from someone I know very well, just saying hello and not much more. She's a very kind woman, but somehow I had so much work to do that I left it to be answered later. My pain was quite strong and was making me uncomfortable. After several hours of this, and since I didn't answer, she called me. The moment that I heard her voice I connected with her and I only asked one thing: are your kidneys ok? "No, I'm in incredible pain and can't even move". That moment when I realized that the pain was not mine, it disappeared. Then I realized that the moment I got the pain was the exact moment she sent me the email. She, thinking of me, and without knowing it, sent me the pain. And I felt it thinking it might have been mine. This is being empathic.

And this process comes through frequency, vibration, the energy that connects us all, like a cosmic nervous system.

Our most energetic spot is located 2 or 3 fingers bellow our navel, inside our body. In Tantra, it's used to recycle and power our sexual energy, that can be used by the brain, to heat, or even to heal. But we have others through which we communicate: usually it's with this one and the one that we commonly call the 3rd eye, which is also inside our body and located on our pineal gland. Two of our main chakras. Than we have another one on the top of our skull that connects us with the Universe: a cosmic gate.
All these spots are in connection with the Universe, thus, with all beings. It's all vibration and frequency that goes through you and through us all. I am energy as you are. I am frequency as you are.
One basic exercise of visualization through meditation that you can do, if you're not experienced in this, is to visualize a flower in front of you: start by visualizing a seed underground. Visualize it opening and searching for light, sending to it a beam of energy from your chakra bellow your navel. "Give birth" to the flower and visualize it now growing up until it blooms as the flower you wanted. Once you "have" the flower in front of you in your visualization, you can now use it to recycle your own energy, sending and receiving. You can create a triangle of energy for example, sending the energy from your navel to the flower

and getting new recycled energy from the flower and send that to your 3rd eye. Give different colours to these beams of energy. Feel the frequency and vibration. If you kill the flower in this process, you can always "give birth" to another one. Visualization of energy is a powerful and unlimited resource. If you need a deeper recycling, visualize a tree, a fruit tree instead.
Create your own source of healing from your own source of energy through visualization.

In Sufism, they dance. They use the energy of sound, the frequency spiralling and manifesting more frequency and resonance. They go through a trance using spiralling energy. Creating and recreating new states of consciousness. New energy and frequency. They dance like Shiva creating spirals of energy. Re-creating. Recycling. Destroying what's no longer useful to give new life. Healing. You recycle what is broken into a new healed energy. Drums can be used, as Tibetan singing bowls can be used to create resonance, existing as one. You and energy are one. You're frequency and resonance, that is why you connect with the drums and Tibetan bowls in your healing practices.

If you want to live in a better world you should work to be better yourself. Like in our democracies every vote counts and you should vote, on a higher level you have also a vote that counts immensely to create a better world. You should think of consciousness not as your own, but as a higher one. And for it, you should use your thoughts; you should work on yourself so you can offer a better slice of consciousness to the cosmic one. The world is now confused, in crisis. People live in fear and with anger. The only and best thing we can do now to heal the world, is to heal ourselves first, so we can contribute with better consciousness to the Universe. It depends on each one of us. You, me, or even that neighbour who doesn't leave us alone. If you send him thoughts of anxiety and anguish, you're sending that unconscious feeling to the Universe, thus, you're sending them back to you. It's the way Universe works: sending back our thoughts. If you send a thought "I want to be better", the Universe will send it back to you: "yes, you want". And it doesn't result in anything. You should instead create an action-thought: "I am better". Being actually better, progressing every day, every moment. And then, the Universe will send it back to you: "yes, you're better". And you can go forward. If you send thoughts of anger towards the Universe, you will most probably receive them back. So be wise, build your being as an altruistic unlimited resource of precious energy. Tune yourself into the resonance of the Earth. Be a tree. Be an animal. Be yourself in the most pure energy and frequency. Connect and be one with the Universe. Be an open channel of energy.

Master yourself. Always remember that we are just bodies of frequency. Like a frail flower is.

When you visualize a flower growing, you should have knowledge of the spiral. The spiral has always been a symbol of growth in most ancient cultures and still is. No matter if it's a symbol from the Incas or the Hindus. You can find spirals all over the world left by the people in the Palaeolithic period, Mongol, Gaelic or Zulu. If you see a flower growing in slow motion, or time lapse, you will notice that they grow in a spiral movement. Like tornados. Creating their own inner energy, thus frequency. It connects Earth to the Heavens. The energetic source and the creative force.

Focus on an energetic spot. Focus on growth. On expanding. When you visualize the beam of energy that you're sending, visualize it as a dynamic spiralling beam. It's not a direct light; it's a spiralling light of energy. It grows and expands spiralling until it reaches the target. So you do the same when healing: You send spirals of energy in beams of light and heat. If it helps you, visualize a spiralling structure of energy similar to the shape of our DNA.

Be the eye of the spiral yourself, the one from which the energy originates and flows. The Universe does the same towards you, whenever you're receptive and opened to it, allowing the same message to manifest within you.

Use this energetic visualization also to protect yourself.

Why meditation though? Although our thinking process as humans can give us a better way to live, as in conformity, it's also what separates us from the Universe, from nature itself. We are educated to think, not to feel anymore. Not to listen or use our most basic senses. In meditation you find silence of mind, there are no thoughts disturbing or cutting our connection with the frequency of Earth. When our minds are silent there is more awareness of the Universe. We connect to our higher self within nature. We become one with the cosmic energy and frequency. There are no thoughts interfering in the process of communication. Thinking is a great skill that we possess as humans, but we must master our own minds. There's space for eating, working, living and sleeping in our lives as human beings on Earth. There should also be space for thinking and for silence of one's mind. To be connected. To be one. To feel what cannot be understood by our thinking process.

Meditation is that: the connection with our higher self, in silence. The higher self that is connected with the Universe, for a better Collective Consciousness, aligning our chakra's meridian, our energetic balance.

For several ancient cultures, thinking was the 6th sense. Following this, you're not what you think because you're not what you smell, or taste. You're a witness of your thoughts like you're a witness of your other senses. The moment you accept this as true, you will start using your thoughts as a tool of your mind, to be used, to witness. To acknowledge them, and not to be driven by them, even less to be enslaved by your own thoughts. And don't deny yourself this because most of us humans, due to our discontent and western education, became slaves to our thoughts. We no longer follow our instincts because we follow what we think. We no longer trust on our senses. It's important then that you use your thoughts as a tool, and not become imprisoned by your mind. And when you use your thoughts as a tool, you will become free, just a witness, with a higher mind able to find your own silence, to connect yourself with the whole, the Universe and the Cosmic Consciousness. Then, you can be master of yourself. Not when you're driven by your thoughts, but when you master them, when you're able to play with them, re-wiring your brain when needed. Meditation is an amazing process to obtain this. To make yourself master of your own mind as meditation will guide you to your higher self and silence. When you find silence, you will manifest control over your thoughts. You will become pure energy, mastering your mind and body.

The brain wires itself according to your thoughts. Or according to your inner silence. You can master your mind with this. You can re-wire it and be master of your own mind. You might have heard several times the expression "mind over matter"… but what's over mind? You. You are the master of your own mind, as I am the master of my own. I am the master of my mind, and my mind then masters the matter. I rewire the mind not to suffer in case I feel pain. And the mind rewires the matter to not feel the pain that otherwise would make me suffer. If you master your mind to feel negativity and suffering, you will feel miserable. Instead, if you rewire your mind to feel compassion, gratitude and joy, you will experience silence and bliss. You will master your own consciousness. You will master your own matter as well. Create your own reality and spread it. Accept yourself and embrace your mind. Find your inner silence and you'll master yourself. This is vital for a healer: to be free of thoughts. Be a channel of energy, open for the Earth and the Heavens. Be truth.

Be consciousness. It's consciousness that is over mind.

And if it's consciousness that creates matter, matter exists as quantum, thus derives from consciousness. Consciousness is part of the quantum and quantum part of the consciousness. It's circle of life itself, because everything in life is consciousness.

Δ

Let's talk about lucid dreams. We all want to be lucid in this life. Aware of the whole as a participant and as an observer. A Lucid dream is when you're aware, lucid, of your own dream. You're dreaming and at the same time you're aware that you're dreaming. You can even control it. And this can be obtained through meditation as well. Ever since I was very young I had several lucid dreams and I still do. But what's the point if we only have lucid dreams for our own pleasure? Lucid dreams can be used to heal others, to help others, to contribute to the cosmic or Collective Consciousness. Yes, you get it real.
Before I continue I want to make clear that in order for you to practice meditation, or even transcendental meditation, you don't need to follow Buddhism, but their teachings and practices can help you. Buddhism is not a religion, it's a philosophy of life, and it's most probably complementary to whichever religion you choose to follow, atheism or even paganism.

Practicing lucid dreaming is a wonderful way to be awake and aware of life. It is also a wonderful tool to heal others. One of the things that can help you go into a lucid dream is wearing headphones and listening to the resonance of the Earth, the frequency waves of the brain. When you're having a regular dream, or nightmare, you have no control. But when lucid dreaming you're not only able to conduct and guide it, but also heal your traumas, phobias, or other issues that you might need to heal. It works like self-hypnosis.

Dreams and nightmares are usually the releasing of your worries by your subconscious. When you're able to guide them you can heal yourself by conducting a self-healing. Exactly like when you practice self-hypnosis, or when you're being guided through hypnosis. Understanding your own dreams is understanding your own consciousness. It's understanding your higher self.

In science, a lucid dream is called "a hybrid state of consciousness". In Tibetan Buddhism, it's just a normal practice that helps us heal and be aware of who we in essence are.

Lucid dreaming can then become a simple way to deal with your own nightmares and dreams. To take advantage of them, to no longer fear your own monsters. To not repress them, but to learn with them instead.

Sleeping takes up a third of our lives. Lucid dreaming is a way to take advantage and make use of that time.

To embrace your own self, your fears, your worries. To be grateful and healed. To be connected with your higher self. A lucid dream comes from wisdom, to increase wisdom. In the shamanic Bon tradition, the Tibetan philosophy that was merged into Buddhism, the lucid dream is an important factor and it's usually achieved from practicing Tantra.

It is important you to understand that the practice of lucid dreaming, although being inner work, is vital for the Collective Consciousness. By constantly purifying and healing ourselves, we are healing the others through Collective Consciousness.

Think about your home, in which you live with others, no matter if they are friends or family. If any of the residents have a bad mood and start shouting at the others, it will create an environment that has bad energy in your home. However, if there's just one person who has a wiser attitude, good will and able to master his own higher self, he can transform that bad energy into a much better one. You can stop an argument or fight between two other people just by taking some distance, going into meditation, finding your inner peace and sharing it telepathically or through the Collective Consciousness, directing it towards the other two people or just creating an harmonious shield protecting the whole house. When you master your mind, you will be able to master your environment. When you master self-healing, you will be able to heal others. Think of energy, be energy and spread it in the wisest and most harmonious way. If you feel that the vibration is lost or in a bad wave, transform it, recycle it visualizing the frequency of the Earth and spread it.

I remember once being at a friends' house for few days, when they had a bad argument in the room next door. It had nothing to do with me so I didn't interfere. I simply sat down, visualized the energy and frequency of the Earth connected to my mind and spread it towards the two of them in the next room. By visualizing them and the Earth's frequency, I made them slowly stop the harsh words they were exchanging, and the tone of it, until they started talking to each other in a more respectful way and finally they were smiling and laughing. But first I cleared my mind, connected myself to Earth and then I visualized the resonance and frequency of nature and directed it towards them.

Growing up in western traditions I often heard those pre-conceived and easy judgmental ideas that in Buddhism we look too much at our own navel. Yes, we look at our inner self, but this is to keep our mind clean so we can spread awareness and healing to the Collective Consciousness. We look at our inner selves in order to keep it clear and healed. If you're ill, you have no strength to act and heal others. You must be clear and healed yourself so you can have strength and power to heal others.

To be useful in our Collective Consciousness. To be one with it. And the way the world now is with the financial crisis, society's greed, etc., we do need to keep our higher selves clear and healed so we can spread it in the most positive and useful way.

If you're tense, dirty and stressed, no one will want to have you hug them because you're the one who needs it. But if you're clean, healthy and healed, all others will be fond of your presence and embrace.

Working with triggers can be quite helpful. As humans, we are often touched or even invaded by less good energies, thoughts, moods. If you pay attention to the moments in which they come to you, you can make them conscious and set off a trigger. In the case I wrote earlier with two of my friends arguing, it came to me as an unbalanced energy of hate by frustration. I don't want that in me, I don't want to feel that, because I know hate and frustration can unbalance one's mind and emotions. What I did some time ago was to make myself conscious of it and create something to trigger it when I'm not protected. I then informed the mind that whenever that specific feeling comes to me it should respond consciously, triggering a deep breath, focusing on the Earth's resonance. When it happened I immediately become aware of it and didn't allow it to invade me, or else I would be influenced by that emotion. It immediately triggered the connection to Earth, so I could focus on peace of mind, and then spread it towards them two.

It's important for you to find ways to set off whenever an undesired emotion comes close to your energetic field. That moment, when you are conscious of it, your mind will set off the trigger so that will react in a better way. When I feel hate, my mind immediately connects with Earth's frequency to give my mind some peace, and then be able to spread it and heal the source. Not only do I keep my mind balanced, but I also heal the source giving equal balance of mind and emotion.

This is a way to protect yourself: control your mind so that you are not affected by the energy of others. Find something that can set off a trigger whenever you're conscious of that energy.

It can also be done for example if you have a moment of anxiety: if you inform your mind that whenever you are anxious it should trigger a deep breath and peace of mind, you will then overcome anxiety. And this works for hate, jealousy, etc.: embrace it and heal the source.

All this requires daily practice, and if you don't have the visualization and healing skills natural within you, even more.

Ever since I was a child, and not even aware of the existence of Buddhism or meditation, I would sit still in the lotus position for an hour or two whenever I was in the countryside. In my mind, sitting still on a rock or under a tree, would be my best disguise and no one would find me. As if I was a chameleon: in my mind I would be the tree or the rock. You can sit by the shade and be the shade, or under the light and be the light.

When you dive naked in the sea you should be as watery as the water itself. Being one, finding the inner silence of the element.

Daily meditation practices can start with controlled time. You may inform your mind that you want to "wake up" half an hour later. And trust your mind with this. Leave it up to your mind.

Everyday my dog comes to me at the same hour. At 7 pm he comes and sits in front of me. He knows it's time for me to give him dinner. He doesn't have clocks or alarms. We, as animals have the sense of time too, so listen to it.

I did the same when I went into brain death: I informed the mind that I wanted to come back after 3 days, and exactly 3 days later I woke up.

Then sit still for that half an hour. Find the silence within you. Relax all your muscles. Visualize and feel the muscles in the face one by one. When you have them all relaxed you will be aware of an inner and peaceful smile. You can practice daily any amount of time you want. Go slowly and

listen to your own body and mind. Feel comfortable and don't listen to anything that can distract you.
When you master meditation, you don't need to sit down like before. Even though I keep doing it as a daily practice, and even when I'm writing I sit down in the lotus position and break the rhythm of the writing to stay still for some moments, most of the time when I am alone I live in constant meditation. I walk, I take a shower, I eat, I write… while in meditation. Some of my daily rituals are moments of meditation, like cooking. Cooking is a creative ritual for me, and I do it most of the times in a meditative state. I empty my mind, and in silence and peace I follow my senses allowing my hands to cook and feel. I often heal others with my meals as well, sharing the meals as healing and cleaning ones. I let myself be guided by the smell of the salt and herbs and food, colours and textures to come up with a meal. For the senses and for the mind.
Find your inner silence and embrace it. In it you will find your own piece of mind, and you will connect to your higher self.

If you find easier you can listen to some music that can ignite your inner silence, and for this there are some frequencies that are better than others, being the shamanic drums or the Tibetan bowls an example. Mongolian throat singing can also trigger a meditative trance.

There was a situation in which I was in trance as if I was induced by hallucinogenic drugs. Like I explained in the book, I wanted to experiment the feeling without the use of drugs. I informed my mind then that I was ready for it and I began reading a book in which the author describes his own experience with Ayahuasca. I allowed his feelings to enter my mind and I experienced it as if I had taken the drugs myself. I went straight into it without problems.

I looked at the window that has my altar to see the moon. I rang the Tibetan bowl in the four directions, Earth and Heavens. The bowl was almost full of water that was left to capture the first light of the full moon. I rang the bowls twice, and a third time, now more energetically, telling the spirit of the jaguar, the animal of the west to come and be in me and help me end the suffering of some people who asked me to heal them, to help and guide me to be a better healer. In some cultures the jaguar is the most powerful animal that lives in the two worlds: the physical and the spiritual. The moment after, I woke up with a strong vibrating sound next to my head. I was lying down on the floor of clay tiles and the whole altar had fallen all over me. Buddha had remained in the same place but was facing west now, from where the Jaguar comes. I fainted and woke up with the sound of the bowl hitting the floor. Or with my head hitting the floor, maybe at the same time as the Tibetan bowl. There I was, waking up from fainting. I realized immediately what had happened and stood up. I felt dizzy and didn't touch anything. I had left the window open on purpose so the shrine would have the first moonlight touching it. But I made a terrible mistake: I didn't protect myself with an energetic shield when I called the spirits. I was too tired and didn't realize that, and the moonlit water from the bowl had showered all over me.

I was very dizzy and sat down on the bed. With incredible difficulty, as if it was the hardest task in the world, I took off my clothing. I was amazed that I was able to do so since everything around me was floating and distorted, even the sleeves of the shirt were endless. As soon as I lay down on my bed I realized that I needed to pee, so I stood up again and went to the bathroom. While peeing I felt a weird force inside of me as if a dark alien was possessing me inside my guts while consuming all my energy. I kept peeing even though I was very dizzy. I woke up on the floor after first hitting my head again on a wooden bench and then on the floor. When I woke up I realized that I was still peeing, lying on the floor, all over myself. I didn't care. I looked at my naked body and at the floor and saw that I was fully wet as well as the floor around me. I thought "I don't care I can clean the floor tomorrow". I went back to bed after drinking a bottle of sparkling water thinking that I would fall asleep perfectly after that. I had found the bed! If I would faint a third time I would at least be lying down on my bed so it wouldn't matter.

I could keep sleeping, because I wouldn't wake up after falling and hitting my shaved head again on the floor of clay tiles. But as soon as I lay down I felt deeply sick with a huge need to throw out that insane alien. I responded fast, covering my mouth with my hands, stood up and ran to the toilet where I could finally vomit my guts out. I knelt as a precaution; if I fainted again I would be closer to the floor. I kept vomiting and then I saw that I was vomiting what seemed to be a whole bush of rosemary. I was vomiting and all the leaves were intact. Rosemary is the plant used to send the bad spirits away, usually used like incense, burned. The stomach was in a struggle with what seemed to be an alien inside trying to survive. But I got rid of the rosemary. And the alien. I flushed, and went to bed after a quick shower. I could finally sleep well and relax now.

The night went on with me struggling because I was becoming conscious of the pain caused by falling twice. I spent all night sleepily conscious of my body and how it was hurting. I touched the back of my head and upper neck to see if it was not bleeding, but it was only swollen and sore. I checked my elbow. I realized that I had also hurt my left knee and my right elbow. Only to realize afterwards, that I must have hurt my whole body when I fell to the floor. Twice. I spent the whole night being conscious of my body as if I was not there though. As if I was next to it, feeling it by empathy. As in a projected lucid dream. All night long I felt split from myself. My body on one side of the bed and on the other side my energetic body, like a spirit of mine. Outside it started raining more violently and I listened to it while I could feel my body aching, free from the consuming alien though. Moving slowly to find better postures I couldn't sleep. I had a conscious sleepless night. It was 6am when I checked the time. I felt good and stood up for my morning coffee. I felt good. Tired, sleepy, but good. As if a deep cleansing had taken place within me. I killed the dark energy with the dagger that I often felt stabbing my head. All that light of the moon, the powerful jaguar making me puke to clean my inner body from some weird energy that was absorbing me. It keeps raining. And the only thing in my mind was the incredible experience I had with hallucinogenic drugs that I didn't take. That cleaned me inside. Vomiting can be very aggressive to the body. I always felt it, as I always felt a cleansing afterwards. I thought that someone close to me had died, and that was what I had felt: her agony leaving this world going through me. Someone had used me as channel to change between worlds. It's 7:30am now and I still didn't know who she was though. Maybe I just got finally released from what has been bothering me and dragging me down for a long time. That was the death feeling: I killed the intruder in me. That's why I felt split afterwards. That's why I feel cleansed and released now.

Δ

Autism has always helped me with shamanism and healing, as shamanism and healing has always helped me with being autistic. Both are part of who I am and I embraced and accepted it a long time ago. As autistic I never had meltdowns but I do have shutdowns, more as a need of existing within my own silence, protected from the world. But the co-existence of both can also be a lifelong battle, which I embraced as well: dealing with being logical and intuitive at the same time.
I feel, I think, therefore I energy.
Thinking is also a process and can be helped by intuition; as intuition can be helped by logical thinking. They both can co-exist helping each other.
Whenever I have a shutdown I trigger logical thinking so I can keep connecting with my self and others if necessary. Sometimes even a simple "hello" from someone else can break my silence and make me agitated, if I'm having a more sensitive day, or in a "shutdown" day. With the help of meditation this is easier to control though. For autistic people, connecting by verbal speech can take a huge amount of energy, making us feel completely drained. It requires an incredible effort, what seems to be nothing to others.
Every morning I try to drink my coffee outside where the morning light can touch me, in the garden or, if I'm in a

flat, on the balcony. After that I start working on whatever project I'm on. Usually with the noise cancelling headphones, listening to Tibetan bowls, Shamanic drums, the Earth's resonance or piano. This keeps my mind and ego out of the way. I remain in a state of early morning trance, connected with my consciousness and higher self. When I'm writing I'm not conscious of what I'm writing: I let it go, I release through my consciousness. It doesn't know names and labels of things. It knows experience and intuition and it has memories directly from my bank of memories untouched by logical thinking or by conscious filters. I don't remember what I write. I just write and let it go. I'm only conscious of what I wrote afterwards when I finish the book, and giving myself some time to not be emotionally connected to it I give myself a chance to read it as if it was written by another author. This was what happened to "The Sacred Book of G" as well: I only read it after it was published. I needed to be emotionally detached in order to read it. This book I will read before publishing it though. I just happened to open the document randomly and found something curious I wrote. I know I will learn from what I wrote when I'm finished and have read this book. The process of being able to learn from ourselves this way is quite interesting. We are who we ought to be. We are the product of the life we have lived as well. The whole experienced life, including all the people we spent time with during our lives. We are the result of the whole.

But we are what we decide to be. We are the only one responsible for our own self. So we can and should learn from ourselves. Letting go through our subconscious is a great process, as most of our thoughts are produced by this filtered consciousness we possess, and most of the time we don't even listen to our higher consciousness or subconscious. It's vital to listen to ourselves and learn from our own mistakes and flaws so we can overcome them and exist in a better way. It's as important to be able to tease yourself as it is to embrace our own flaws. To be aware and conscious of them, to accept, in order to progress and move forward. Whenever you're stuck in your past and flaws, you're not able to progress and move on. Accept, embrace, and forgive yourself. With all the flaws you might have. Tease yourself with them, play with them. Only that way you can overcome them.

Δ

Think on a larger scale and be aware that you're just a tiny piece of energy in our Multiverse. Centuries ago we thought that Earth was the centre of the Universe. Then we discovered that the sun was the centre. Afterwards we found a galaxy. And another. And another. Now, finally, scientists are accepting the fact that there's not only our Universe but also several others. It's the concept of Multiverse. Parallel Universes co-existing in space and time. For us, that star we see is already dead. It only exists in our space and time. For any other planet we might be dead already, or yet to be born. We keep worrying about our own navels, family, friends, neighbourhood, city, and country. But we should have a conscious concept of the Multiverse and how small we are and how we can influence the whole. It seems contradictory, but we can. Each one has an important mission in this life on Earth. Our thoughts are part of a bigger scheme of things. We exist, we live, we think. We feel and we're beings of energy within this Multiverse. Your actions not only contribute directly to your own life but to the Collective Consciousness. You are whom you decide to be, the only one responsible for your own actions and life. You're energy within the energy. You're the result of a smaller big bang, which expanded to give birth to yourself. And your consciousness is the only one responsible for who you now are. If you think negatively you will get negativity. If you don't trust yourself that's the energy you spread in the Universe. So we should accept ourselves, improve it every moment, and spread awareness and acceptance and positivity. But to spread those positive thoughts and energy we ought to be one with it. We must work on ourselves so we can share who we are the best way we can. If you're ill you cannot heal. If you're negative you can't help others to overcome their issues because you'll be spreading negativity.

You should improve yourself to share that energy, to be better, to get better in return. You must trust yourself in your purest of thoughts and emotions.

You lived your past, but you don't own it. It's past already. You are as I am, you are not the past: you are the now. And being in the now you're taking a step towards who you will be. Release the past because it's not yours. Release the thoughts, as you don't own them either. The only thing you own is the now, the present moment, your now action. You were responsible for your past when it was now, but it is no longer, so you should release it to where it belongs: past experience. Use it to learn, not to carry on your shoulders. Learn and move on. Don't get stuck. Forgive yourself as you forgive others.

André Malraux wrote once that "death changes life into destiny", to add "and when man faces destiny, the destiny ends and man comes to his own". And this is important, to change our destiny, the fear of death, or the concept that death is our ultimate journey in which we are finally able to meet our higher self. You can face your destiny, first by being aware, then by acting accordingly. Meditation can lead into it helping you to connect with your higher self. You can't live forever as appearance; you should live coherently with your deepest self. Working your inner self towards the higher self, in which there's no ego.

I just had to stop writing because I suddenly lost my eyesight seeing only blind spots and flashlights. I closed my eyes and there was one image only: a mountain with a river underneath flowing with a second river coming from the right: a river of blood. A vision that came from nowhere and I'm not yet aware of the meaning of it. When I opened my eyes though, my friend was standing in front of me, sign-gesturing if I wanted some tea. But the moment I saw her, I also saw the spirit of a man leaving her body towards the window. I shall pass and not allow my mind to get disturbed or to carry it: as always the meaning will come to me, or somehow I will be able to understand. The Universe often manifests in curious and creative ways, usually through Cosmic Consciousness, to the Collective Consciousness, until it reaches our higher consciousness if you have open channels.

Moments before an earthquake the animals feel it and react. We are the last ones to react because we live in a mind-ego-logical state that cuts us off from our connection to the Earth. But if you work on opening your energetic channels you will feel and understand it better. You're just energy with a body of matter. You're nothing but an energetic carrier of consciousness. You own nothing, although you're the only one responsible for your own actions. You can use them wisely, or remain ignorant; be altruistic or remain egocentric and selfish.

If you have the skills and knowledge to allow your energetic channels to be wiser you will be able to use them to heal others, keeping yourself healed. You're nothing, but you can use your nothingness as open channels to provide the Collective Consciousness with healing and positive energy whenever you're one with nature and your higher self. You're just a channel between the Earth and the Heavens, you can and should use it wisely, taking action and being aware of that. Your past is not yours, you are now. The past only built your foundations.

Do not fear death: live life and allow yourself to be a tool for the Universe. Be humble because the Universe is the best teacher and tutor and you can only learn by listening to it. Being ready and open to it. Being awake.

Since a long time ago I plant a tree every year. It's a ritual of my own, an offer to Earth expressing my gratitude for life and for its teachings. But there is a special tree I planted in the ground of the country house of my family. Somehow I feel more connected with it. I am the tree. Interestingly enough, the tree only produces fruit whenever I'm there. If I spend a year without going there, the tree doesn't produce fruit. In the years I go there, the tree gives an incredible amount of fruit. I am that tree. The tree is me. You too are a tree. Whenever you feed yourself, being connected, you're your higher creator, and you're able to be fruitful. Whenever you're not connected to yourself and

to the Earth's resonance, you're useless and you will not be able to be fruitful. You must feed your higher self, instead of feeding your ego. Be awake in order to be fruitful.
When you water a rose you don't spread water over its petals: you feed its roots so the petals can shine.
You feed its roots so the rose can exist. And this is what you should do with yourself. Feed your higher and inner self in order to exist. To bloom. If you only feed your ego, your roots will dry out and the flower will die too. A flower is a visible channel between the Earth and the Heavens. It has roots, and the deeper they are the more chances it has to survive in all its fullness. A flower grows towards the Heavens, in spiral, so it can be blessed by the Sun. We too must exist this way: feeding our roots, our existence, growing in a spiral towards the Heavens. Like any other body of energy. And if you're blessed with consciousness, you must come down to earth and learn from the most fragile of plants. Then you can look and learn from the cactus and how it deepens its roots and how it keeps a reservoir for times of drought. And they co-exist, roses and cactus. As we should do with each other.
When you're living in the past, what you're really doing is removing your present, thus your own future. Living the present though, is what makes you closer to eternity.

Oliver Sacks came to mind after this episode of flashlights and blind spots followed by a vision. He explains that hallucinations can be a first signal of migraines. And how true and visionary can a hallucination be? He writes in his latest autobiography "I have been able to see my life as from a great altitude, as sort of landscape, and with a deepening sense of the connection of all its parts". This is very important, and this I learned to do after my brain death episode: to actually be able to see your life from a greater altitude with a deep sense of connection to the whole.

When my friend came immediately after me having this vision, I understood that the river of blood came from her, and that the flowing river was from me. I was embracing her suffering, as she later told me what happened right before. Then I could heal her, being conscious of the source. If you look your life and the life of your environment from a greater altitude it is far easier to understand the whole. Being connected.

You do. Go into meditation or into trance and visualize yourself from an eagle's point of view. You will be able not only to see yourself within the surroundings, but also to see you out of yourself, and how you're behaving and how your thoughts towards you and others are. You will see the big picture of your life. Rewind and forward. Pay attention to all the details you see. The eagles, like other birds, fly in a spiral when they want to hunt. Do it yourself and fly around in spiral so you can focus on who you are in the big picture.

It's a deep and magical moment if you're able to do that. It happened to me for the several hours in which I was in a coma right before the 3 days of brain death. I was "awarded" with this sight: my whole life in a movie seen from the Heavens. It will make you think and change for a better connection with the whole. For a better understanding of life and of light.

Whenever you praise the Sun and the Earth and the Heavens, you're disconnecting yourself from them. Instead you must be Sun, Earth and Heavens. One with them. Connected to your higher self, and ultimately to the Cosmic Consciousness.

"Matter is created from the original and eternal energy that we know as Light. It shone, and there have been appear star, the planets, man, and everything on the Earth and in the Universe. Matter is an expression of infinite forms of Light, because energy is older than it. There are four laws of Creation. The first is that the source of all the baffling, dark plot that the mind cannot conceive, or mathematics measure. In that plot fit the whole Universe.

The second law is spreading a darkness, which is the true nature of Light, from the inexplicable and it's transformed into the Light. The third law is the necessity of the Light to become a matter of Light. The fourth law is: no beginning and no end; three previous laws always take place and the Creation is eternal." Wrote Tesla.

In the same interview, Tesla confirms that most of his inventions and creations came from lucid dreams and visualizations.

Humans are too attached to matter. They don't understand the source of it, thus of themselves. They see the superficial form, visible to the earthly eyes. They are attached to things, including their own physical bodies. They exist not questioning. They are fulfilled with their own existence as it is.
Whenever we go deeper, we understand the source of life, or of energy itself and we will no longer fear death, because we will understand that death is being detached from a material shape. Humans fear this: the loss of matter. Of being light. So they praise it, keeping it at a distance. Giving to the light the name of the gods. As if they were not gods themselves. They are. We all are. Some are just more awakened then others. Less attached to matter, knowing that energy is the only source of life.
There's this humanity's greed of mater, of body, and of

shape, only because most men don't go deeper, thus they live in fear of loss. The moment you become the essence, the energetic channel between the Earth and the Heavens, you will no longer fear death because you will finally understand the meaning of life. Which for most, is only attainable when they die. And because humans are energy in a body of matter, they are narcissistically and greedily in need of more matter.

Meditation helps you in this process: you don't get rid of your body of matter; you just learn how to use it, instead of being used by it. You'll be aware of the energy within you, the only creator of yourself: your only existence. They don't seek to transcend the human gnosis. They exist in their greedy attachment to matter.

Asked what Cosmic pain is, Tesla answers:

" We are on Earth… It is an illness whose existence the vast majority of people is not aware of. Hence, many other illnesses, suffering, evil, misery, wars and everything else what makes human life an absurd and horrible condition. This disease cannot be completely cured, but awareness shall make it less complicated and hazardous. Whenever one of my close and dear people were hurt, I felt physical pain. This is because our bodies are made as of similar material, and our soul related with unbreakable strands.

Incomprehensible sadness that overwhelmed us at times means that somewhere, on the other side on this planet, a child or generous man died.

The entire Universe is in certain periods sick of itself, and of us. Disappearance of a star and the appearance of comets affect us more than we can imagine. Relationships among the creatures on the Earth are even stronger, because of our feelings and thoughts the flower will scent even more beautiful or will fall in silence.

These truths we must learn in order to be healed. Remedy is in our hearts and evenly, in the heart of the animals that we call the Universe."

Through transcendental meditation you can finally understand the real concept of space and time, being and not being. You will experience an out of body moment, in which you're able to be aware of the energy, your own source of consciousness. You will be one within the Universe then. Experiencing death is then not more than facing and understanding the source of life itself. It is being detached from matter, being energy, connected to the Universe by its own frequency. It's being vibration, a manifestation of energy towards matter.

Only then you will live, awaken.

Not following the energy: just being it.

Δ

Nature, both in life and death, has taught me that each moment is unique in our learning process. All my life on Earth I've been listening to reason and intuition. With both listening to each other. With both blaming each other. My logical thinking gives reason to my intuition. As I live. Or as I allow myself to live and learn and listen, being just a channel of energy: a beam of light connecting the Earth and the Heavens. Just like you.

Listen, learn and live.
As Tesla said: "Everything is Light".
And that includes you too.

Δ

I slept all night as I was dreaming and
I dreamt all night as I was sleeping.
Of Magnolias.
A never-ending field of magnolias and I,
Dancing around them all,
Never-ending magnolia field of white flowers,
Edible, smooth tepals touching my naked skin,
Whispering to each other wisdom
Thoughts of intemporality to stay
As secrets of inner satisfactions of being.
Dreams interconnected
From dancing around to becoming one
Magnolia communication as learning how to walk
And being there, and being one.
I slept and dreamt all night that I was in a magnolia field
Of white flowers to become one before I woke up to see the sun.
I am a magnolia tree was how I woke up and the sun smiled.
The wind. It was the wind that brought me the scent.
Warmth by the sun
Blooming all the white petals touching my naked skin.
I woke up as a magnolia tree,
and I dreamt all night that I was just another human.
Blooming.
Another magnolia tree with white flowers of intemporality.

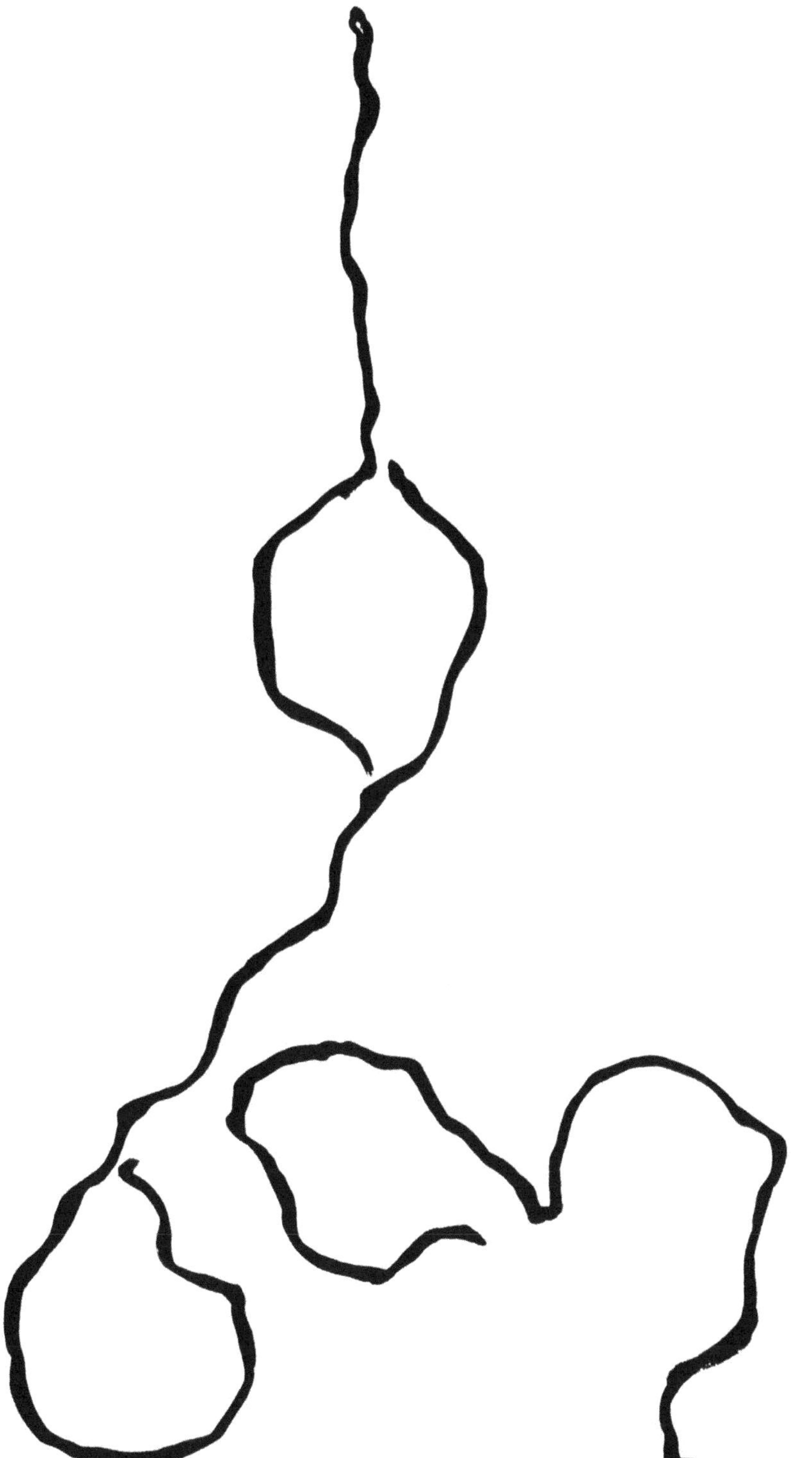

Life is not randomly happening to you: Life is responding to you.
Through consciousness, you can make life happen your way.

Δ

If you look at a crystal, you will notice that if you emanate light onto it, the crystal will reflect and refract, spreading even more light towards you and others. If you're just a dark spot, the crystal can't reflect anything and will remain transparent so you can find the doors of light itself.

Δ

I was born and soon enough being taught that I couldn't be me. That I had to be someone else or someone who would fit and be equal to all the "normal" others. And so I did. I created defences and façades to tease the whole circle-circus of people who demanded me to not be me. I kept dreaming because my mind was my real universe. And that was what made me keep living, I admit, superior minded towards the others because I could do something that they couldn't: live immensely in my own mind, aware of my own consciousness. I was deaf and mute to others' words about gods and dogmas and societies that were built by man who decided how we all should be. As if the beauty of life doesn't contain of differentness and diversity. How unfortunate they were, how frustrated and small minded. Who in his own mind would want to have loud minded creatures nearby when one could chose silence and peace to read and learn and be oneself. I've never been empathic with child-minded, not even when I was one because I never understood them or their need to put down others to feel superior themselves. When they bullied or harassed me, I would look at them thinking how well they would fit silently in one of those large jars at the biology lab like human pickles next to the snakes and other reptiles with their guts out floating in formol. That's how I liked to see them at the time: whenever one would try to bully me, I would imagine them as one of those pickles while looking at them making movements with their mouths in silence because my mind was already disconnected, dreaming and creating my own universes in silence. They were all drowned the moment they would talk to me. It was the only way I could handle them in my sight. I tried to imagine the harassing adults as books though so I could learn from them, but I couldn't stand their dark grey scent as they weren't really books and I loved the smell of books, which is yet to be named. I tried to visualize them as brains then, but their energy was perversely rotten and I couldn't stand their touch or even their patronizing presence. So I remained silent in my secret corners at the Jesuit's school, at the very end of the library to where I would sneak like a snake between shelves to not be seen as if I was a book myself amongst others. I was caught there a couple times though - missing imposed religion or team-sports' classes -, so I soon realized that the concept of safe place didn't exist at all. Or it did, but just in concept. And that was what made me keep living inside my mind, my most secret and safest place on this world in which I lived without being licensed to be me. I never felt lonely though. I have friends and I like to be with myself. And lovers and friends that do not exist either, as they are only projections of what we think so I could keep them inside my mind. But that is what the people who fit in society call crazy because they have no skills to dream and to leave as a dreamer's keeper like I do. I now feel that I spent a large part of my childhood and teenage years running away from people and trying to find my own silence. So I could be me, within nature. I admired free animals and forests. I wanted to be a tree when I grew up. Trees are wiser than most people.

I was born to dream and to live in my mind because the whole world outside of it never made any sense. People talk loud and shit and nonsense because they like to listen to themselves but I'm the crazy one because I don't shout that it is raining when it is. Or when it is not. I can make rain in my mind whenever I want as I can create sunshine in my dream without becoming blind.

On my first day of school I was asked to draw my family. I was 5 years old. I drew all my family naked with little penises and little boobs. In my mind we humans were all equal so I didn't understand the need to make them different. The teacher called the priest director who called my father to complain because they got worried if I was living in a proper family. She then asked me to draw my house, and I drew a big Saturn with its rings filling most of the paper… and Pluto, smaller in size at the top left corner. A dot. The teacher then, curious if I was doing something not that proper again asked me what that dot was and I said it was home. She didn't know that I was coming from Pluto. My father never told them that I came from a lost civilization that was not part of the established academic program. She decided not to ask me to draw under themes anymore. She focused on teaching me how to write, but that I already knew. My first school year became free for me to do what I wanted, so I read most of the time, and drew. I liked science, so I mostly drew scientific things or thoughts to be visualized easier so I could keep the image in my mind.

Today I woke up analysing a pyramid, calculating the angles and sides of it. Even before coffee. It was the only thing I liked to draw when I was a child: triangles and pyramids linked to each other on perfectly round planets. I never understood why my colleagues liked to kick balls though. It's called football. I would look at the ball as if it was a planet and I would think if was inhabited by very little people and how many of those little people would be smashed by their feet kicking the balls. I always imagined everything inhabited by little people and little creatures, so little that we couldn't see them unless with proper glasses on. Later on I discovered microscopes so I could see them. But there were creatures smaller or bigger than others, as I remember to look on the back of the big radio through the holes to find where the singers were hidden. I was born to create worlds with invisible people. Not that I never liked people, I just liked the idea of them being invisible and mute. So I could be me and draw whatever I wanted and read and walk and fly.
Since I was born I was taught to not be me so I learned

how to dream and create and live in my most secret and safest place on Earth.

Eventually I grew up, my body changed and I like to pinch my left nipple whenever I need to come out from my mind. Later on I kept visualizing people still in jars filled with formol. I like the glass between bodies and the touch of it. I like people underwater submerged in silence. I like people in showers and baths. Some people should remain inside water jars. Not touching, not shouting, not even moving. Where they can see me ignoring not touching whenever I would pass in front of their jars. Naked and safe inside my own untouchable and secret mind. But the jars had to be very well closed so the smell of the formol wouldn't come out. I don't like smells, most of them that is. However, whenever I needed to feel safe out of my mind, I would search for an old library for the smell of old books. Curry makes me feel home as well though, yet not as safe as an old book.

I remember for many years I practiced not breathing underwater in swimming pools or even in the bathtub. I enjoy the silence underwater. But I never felt safe there. There were too many people floating underwater for me to feel safe.

In my mind there are no people floating. I prefer people to be in jars instead of being inside of the walls. Walls can hear, they say. And I don't like pickles.

**So I grew wings, letting go of the past I was dragging, becoming safe in my own self.
And that day I became free.**

When I realized that was me, the one living in a jar of formol all these years, I broke my own jar, the one where I was living. Now I fly, I walk and I swim. Invisible whenever I want.
Sometimes randomly just following my consciousness.
Or feeling the winds from the East and South, as they are warmer.

I became free when I realized that I was supposed to be guided by my own inner light, by my own consciousness, no matter by whom I would be surrounded. I became free the moment I cleared myself, not trying to follow, but to be who I am.
And it was only then that my true journey began.

Δ

I healed myself the moment I forgave myself and embraced my past. But it is not me who heals others; it would be arrogant of me to think that. I just happen to have opened energetic channels through which the consciousness runs free, where the spirits of nature co-exist. I am just a medium, a translator, connecting them to others or to myself.

Knowing and having consciousness of oneself is wonderful, it's a first step, and that can be achieved through meditation, through inner silence, through love. Through our deepest connection to nature itself.

The moment we are born is probably the most traumatic one in any being's life. It is also the most wonderful or magical one, in which the physical body connects with its own consciousness. You either embrace the pain to achieve peace with yourself, or you might deal with suffering and mind noise that is what ego brings.

Ego separates body, mind and consciousness. But consciousness can connect them all. It depends on you the one you choose to feed.

If you focus on your body you're focusing on a temporary ego. You will suffer by watching it aging and stress. If you focus on your consciousness you will find a challenging peace, silence and life itself. You will find wisdom from the knowledge of both mind learning, memories from this life and past ones and eternity. Through anamnesis.

I heal myself by being grateful every morning when I wake up and watch the sunrise. I heal myself by being able to hug and wish a good day to all my plants and see them growing and witness their blooming. I heal myself by

being grateful by sending telepathic love onto others. By doing so I heal myself by being grateful for what I receive in return. Light, life, wisdom, peace, silence.
By being connected to earth and heavens.

For that, you must always be working on yourself, learning and listening from every culture, so you can share your best, and know what you can or shouldn't absorb from others. For keeping your consciousness active and clean, in peace with your own self, so you can connect with the collective consciousness, keeping yourself and others healed. In peace.

Δ

According to Plato, Anamnesis is the recollection of the ideas, which the consciousness had known in a previous existence. I went through this process a few times in this life. After the episode of my three days of brain death, one day I felt the need to understand my birth. I went into transcendental meditation and with the help of self-hypnosis, I did a regression in life. At that time I was mainly intrigued by the fact that I never felt comfortable wearing things or being held by my wrists. And somehow I related it with my birth. After a while I saw myself coming out from mother's womb and being held by a tall, bald English man with very light blue eyes. While he was holding me I went into a semi-coma: my body rejected my mother's blood. Incompatibility with her. He then put me in a tight shaped bed, tied my wrists and ankles, and I was immediately tubed to have my first blood transfusion. My first three weeks of life were spent trying to create my own blood. Five total transfusions and two more partial ones. I was rejecting them all. Until I fixed it. The day I was born was in fact three weeks later after birth, the day that the doctor died. The doctor who brought me to life. I remember everything in detail, and by doing this self-hypnosis and transcendental meditation, I healed my past since the moment of my birth. He never gave up on me, and I know now that he gave me his own blood in my last transfusion. His blood became my own and I will be forever grateful to him.

Since that self-healing episode I am no longer uncomfortable being held by my wrists. I know now it was to give me life.

And this led me to think how many people are still holding childhood traumas just because they are ignorant of what happened to them. A well guided hypnosis by someone you trust can be wonderful, if you don't know how to do it yourself. Transcendental meditation can be a tremendous help as well, connecting to your inner self, in silence, apart from the collective energy and disconnected from your own brain, leaving space for your mind to listen to your own consciousness.

Consciousness travels through a cosmic space and time to give life to a new born baby. It is the consciousness who chooses the baby, not the other way round. Consciousness is a gift, an honour, a responsibility. Maybe too much for most people though.

When you're able to connect in silence to your own consciousness and actually listen to it, you'll be able to be one with nature, with collective consciousness, with cosmic consciousness in its own grandeur. You'll be able to better understand old civilizations, your past lives, your own self. Then you will be one, and you'll finally find the deepest respect for all sentient beings. For humanity, for matters of life and death. And finally, you will no longer fear death, so you can enjoy life as it is. Being water, fire, earth and air. Being connected to your inner self.

This is the main reason I took time to write this book, to share knowledge and experience with you. To share life, so you can heal your own self, being free. So you can embrace your own self, body, mind and consciousness.

Δ

I knew how to read and write when I was 5 years old, and I became fascinated with those encyclopaedias for children. I wanted to find answers to everything, real ones. I started with the "how does it work" but that one was more about things made by men, like phones and radios and boats. Only after I got new ones for my birthday, more into universe and cosmos, to later on new ones about civilizations. When I was seven years old I was addicted to planets and forests and stones. I collected all the articles in magazines and newspapers about it and filled a big trunk with all of them. My first collection. The Amazon forest was a big hit for me as I soon found it to be the wisest place nature created on Earth. Forests always fascinated me, and it was my biggest dream to "own" one, so we can have one preserved. It still is.

When I was seven years old my father was called again to the catholic school because I had an argument with the teacher of religion, since what she was saying didn't make any sense, so I explained to her that heaven and hell didn't exist like in catholic dogmas, and that when we would die our body would become part of the earth again, and our consciousness would leave to a cosmic retreat to become pure again to come to another new born some days later. The consciousness would chose the next baby born. And that we are consciousness now living in a body. I explained to her what reincarnation was, even though I never learned about it. I didn't call by its name, the theory just came to my mind as if it was my own. I told her that the idea was brought by my consciousness, through anamnesis, not a thing created by my mind.

Later on I had problems with philosophy classes because they are classes not to philosophize but to memorize their selected philosophers and the catholic priests opinions about them, so I would fail if I would dare to disagree, or even invited to leave the class or put in the punishment room, which was the empty library. Those punishments that I liked, even though the punishment was given for the wrong reasons but by that time I already knew that I couldn't be me. So I danced. And jumped out of the windows to the gardens. To the gardens where I could feel secure. Where I would learn much more from the trees. Much more than with the opinionated priests preaching non-sense after non-sense with their imaginary friend.

Consciousness, - or the awareness of it -, and the anamnesis thing was giving me too many problems in society. So I was mute and deaf most of the time, living in my own silence, connecting with nature to listen to myself. I kept observing humans though, as a rare and weird species because I simply didn't understand why they didn't understand such basic things. Why they would prefer to listen and follow others instead of listen and following themselves.

At the age of thirteen I was taken to the psychologist of the catholic school, which I remember well was a series of exercises and talks that made even less sense. I told her that I couldn't stand noise, and loud minds, and smells, and lights… And she told me I was just shy so she forced me to play drums in the noisiest way possible. I told her again that I wouldn't do that because I would prefer silence. She said I couldn't prefer silence and that I should play drums to create even more noise. She told me then to look at a mirror and find the real me, that I was just one more boy like any other and like others I should make noise and shout and play football and be thankful to their god for having given me life. "Do you understand that the only thing you want me to do is to play silly?" I asked her. I don't want contact with others, I do enjoy my own silence and solitude. "You can't", she replied. She then wrote on a paper and labelled me: "autistic". They put me through psychology tests, and checking my grades they didn't understand, because for them, autism was like being "retarded". If you're not social, if you like your inner silence, and worst of all if you don't believe in their god… That's what you are. But the tests showed that my IQ was the highest, so they had just one label for me: weird. Later on it became High Functioning Autism. Or Asperger. You know how people like labels and follow streams. I never needed any of these labels to understand myself. But they were happy with that, and that made me learn and work on compassion as well. So in fact I was learning with them all. Compassion. Forgiveness. Love.

I'm not sure though if I learned this with people or if they just triggered my consciousness to pick up these things through a process of anamnesis. Collecting data from previous lives through consciousness. The feeling I had that I already knew that information, and just had to know when to apply it.

I feel that I spent most of my youth searching for things that were not supposed to be found. When we started having history classes, and later on art history, I tried to make sense of it, but the movements and periods and eras just didn't fit. Something was lacking, and even more obvious that something was missing was the learning program. Modernism followed by classic Egypt, followed by Gothic, followed by Paleolithic… There was no flowing. Everything in classes were just boring because I was not learning it properly: classes were made for us to memorize and not question it. For my systematic question on "why?" I had always the same answer: "because it is in the books and I say so". Nothing makes sense when you're imposed to memorize things that make no sense by themselves and you don't have answers other than imposed dogmas. So I kept searching outside the box. I learned that people don't know how to have a no as answer, and that for them it is important to win. So I played with them, losing the games on purpose to make them feel happier or better than they were. I still play this game daily so people can be happier thinking they're better. I know, there's a word for that: patronizing. But they don't care as long as they feel good with themselves. For most, the win is more important because they didn't find yet the main purpose of life. They don't understand that one can learn with each other, that an argument can, or should be, a moment of learning, never a game of who wins. We both win, if an argument is interesting. We can all learn with each other, if you listen to others, if you listen to your inner self, if you keep your mind clean with the awareness of consciousness. Why is there a period or an era in the history of the world that was erased as if it never existed if it was obvious that it happened. Why do people want to keep us ignorant when we can learn and become better humans with more knowledge and wisdom? Why can't we just be different and share the diversity as a wonderful way of living? If we are all different. If diversity is wonderful. If we wouldn't learn and grow wiser being all equally close minded. Why are we not allowed to ask different questions in our life on earth, with our own learning process. We now live in an era in which philosophers are no longer accepted or they have to become mainstream and say clichés over and over to be accepted. I've never been sorry for who I am. I just allow myself to be me. My bad days are when I lose patience, because there's too much imposed social thought that I can't handle.

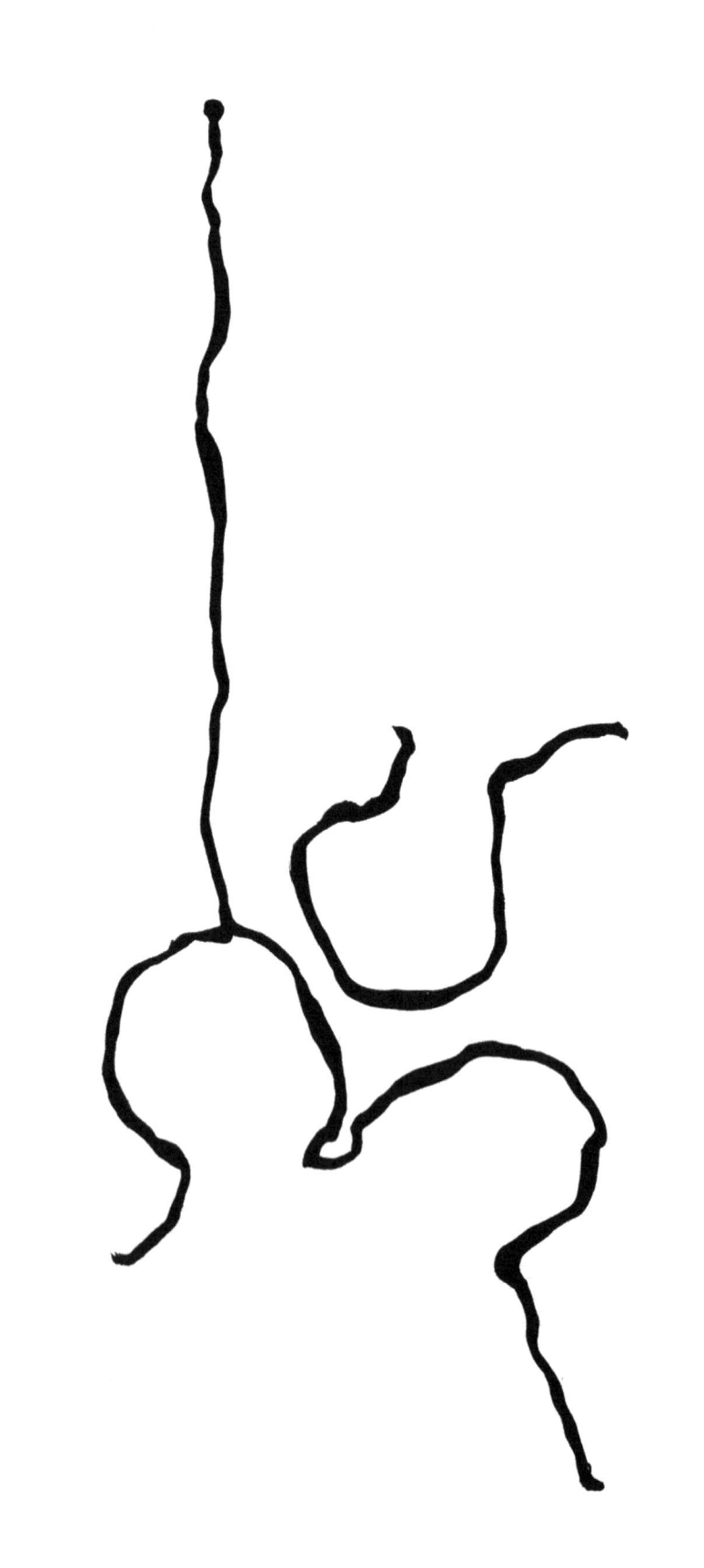

And this is what happens when you deal with an autistic meltdown: we can't deal with loud minds imposing their own mind noise over us.

There are several answers. Silence, Consciousness, Love, Respect, Forgiveness and Compassion are some of them. Sometimes you do have to learn how to be "deaf" and "mute" to let it go. Meditation – and on a deeper level Transcendental Meditation -, is a great way to start. Just focus on your deep breath. Silence your mind to silence the noise out and inside of you. Listen to your intuition, to your consciousness instead of your own mind. Just take a deep breath and feel your own roots. Your own self roots and how they can be fed with a cleaner energy to bloom stronger and healthier.

Δ

My physical self was born in Lisbon. North of the city, there's a place called Sintra. Hills, magical hills, often related to many sources of spirituality. At the hills, if you dare yourself to take a walk at a full moon day through the forest, you might not see much, except some beams of moonlight, but you here and there you can hear some chants from sacred rituals, mostly pagans, to the moon, or to the sun, or other deities. It is a magical place where anything can happen. Since a long time ago Druids and

Pagans, Buddhists and White Magicians and many others gather there for their own sacred rituals. They co-exist together in a respectful way.

I did that once, invited by someone I met at the time, a druid, who asked me to go with him for a special ceremony at the top of the hills. I had just arrived from my years in the Himalayas where I spent my time in a monastery school of philosophy and up in the higher lands with Tibetan Bon Shamans. He was wearing his druid's cape, I wore my Buddhist robes. For an hour we walked on the path to the higher spot, accompanied by chants of different rituals from both sides, once in a while touched by beams of moonlight. We arrived at the highest spot, a stone, like a massive slab and we sat down. We didn't exchange a word that night. We sat down and we started a meditation session, each of us by ourselves, but uniting consciousness, building a stronger collective consciousness.

We'd met a week before. I was having dinner at a small restaurant with friends when he arrived with his group and sat at another table across the room. I looked at him and couldn't see his face. I closed my eyes and opened again trying to focus on him, but I couldn't see anything else than a wolf's head in a human's clothes. I tried to focus once again and again and the only face I could see was the wolf. So I gave up, smiling. Later on, when we finished, I stood up and half way to the exit he stood up too and out of the blue he invited me to be on that place in the hills of Sintra at the next full moon. I don't remember any conversation except a brief "Full moon. Sintra. Hills. South entrance. Wear your ritual robes."

I never saw him again, never knew his name. But the moment we spent together there in meditation, was a wolf's meeting by the full moon.

For many years, maybe through all my childhood and teenage years, I had this recurring dream, in which I was running non-stop, at the top of the hills, in circles, around and around, until I would wake up sweating. Not running alone though, but running away from a wolf that was always by my side. Yes, by my side. And so many times we run away from things that we think they are trying to catch us, not understanding that they are there to be embraced, that in fact they are by our side and not trying to "bite" us. This meeting ended my recurrent dream. This meeting made me realize that I was not being chased, but accompanied. That the wolf by my side was a friend who was there protecting me.

So many times we take others as enemies instead of accepting and embracing them. So many times we run away from our inner selves afraid of ourselves, instead of embracing who we are. Just listen to you, just be silent.

Embrace yourself no matter what. We are all different and it's in our own diversity that the beauty of life lies. Embrace your own wolves. Embrace your own obstacles like a river that embraces the stones and rocks that are on its way, polishing them and letting it go, flowing as if there was no end. Just flowing. And embracing whatever comes your way.

Take time for yourself, accept and embrace the silence. Do not accumulate noise in your mind. Keep it clean. Recycled. So you can find your own silence. So you can find your own consciousness. So you can find your own place in life.

Δ

My consciousness, like yours or anyone else's, is connected to collective consciousness, which is connected to cosmic consciousness. The moment you understand the connection, you're able to communicate. Some people when facing someone else with a different language, instead of trying to understand, listen and learn the other's language to be able to communicate, just shout their own language. They only speak louder, which leads nowhere. Other people try to understand the other's language, to listen, to learn. Those people end up establishing a good communication with the other.

Since childhood I had the need to lie down on the ground (especially in forests or on top of a hill), close my eyes and feel the resonance and vibration of the earth. To be connected you need to feel and listen to her "heartbeat", her breathing. I discovered when I was very young one precious thing: I am made of the same energy as the Earth, which is made of the same energy as the cosmos. The resonance and frequency of my brain is the same as the Earth itself. So I feel her, I listen to her, I learn constantly with her. We learned how to communicate with each other. We are one. And that is what connects me empathically to other people, and to the cosmos itself. What scientists discribe as dark matter, is the same as our mind: a field of energy resonanting in a specific frequency. Our brain has exactly the same frequency as the Earth.

What happens is that most people are too busy and their minds are too loud to connect with Earth itself. And that's why the spiritual awakening is so important, so that people can be in tune with others and with the Earth. That's what I always try to do: spread that knowledge for a better awakening of others. The more people are awakened, the stronger the collective consciousness.

*"Soul receives from soul that knowledge, therefore not by book nor from tongue.
If knowledge of mysteries comes after emptiness of mind, that is illumination of heart."* Wrote Rumi.

Δ

The old civilizations knew this because they had a stronger and deeper connection with the Earth and the Cosmos, especially the shamanic cultures, that existed in different forms in different places. There are shamanic traditions from Mongolia and Tibet, from all over Africa, and from South and Central America. But we must not forget the wonderful connection that Native Americans had as well. And then, there's still the lost civilizations that were never included in our history books, the ones that connected the Earth and all its continents. A supreme civilization with the most amazing connection between Earth and Heavens. A Cosmic one. A civilization that I believe gave birth to the classic Egypt, and later vanished from Earth: The Gobekli Teple, or the cradle of gods, which is now known to have been built 7.000 thousands of years before Stonehenge. Maybe the same age as the Sphinx and Pyramids.
For historians and archeologists, - note that none of them are science -, this has to be a fight, because it might be a matter of stubborn ego… If it is proven right, they would have to unlearn everything they know and start again. They

fail to understand and acknowledge this lost information…
Or did they just erase it because it would be too much for them to discover a lost civilization that was wiser than us? Or as some major politicians say, the world is not prepared for evidence of aliens. Aren't we? Deep down we all know they're here, closer than we might know. Or are they the ones not prepared to leave their own way of doing things? Why are people so distracted by these matters, as if they would live forever in a silly season?

Pyramids were an important connection, a higher altar to consciousness, to collective consciousness and to cosmic consciousness. And not only Pyramids in Egypt but all over the world.
Please answer me if you know: Why do historians, archaeologists, politicians, etc. have the need to keep it wrong and out of context? Why do the established religions have the need and the power to keep humanity divided in the name of the imaginary gods they believe in? Why is so much time needed for people to awaken and allow themselves to connect with our own Nature, Earth, and Cosmos?
Most important of all: what are YOU waiting for to allow yourself to listen to nature? To be nature itself.

Δ

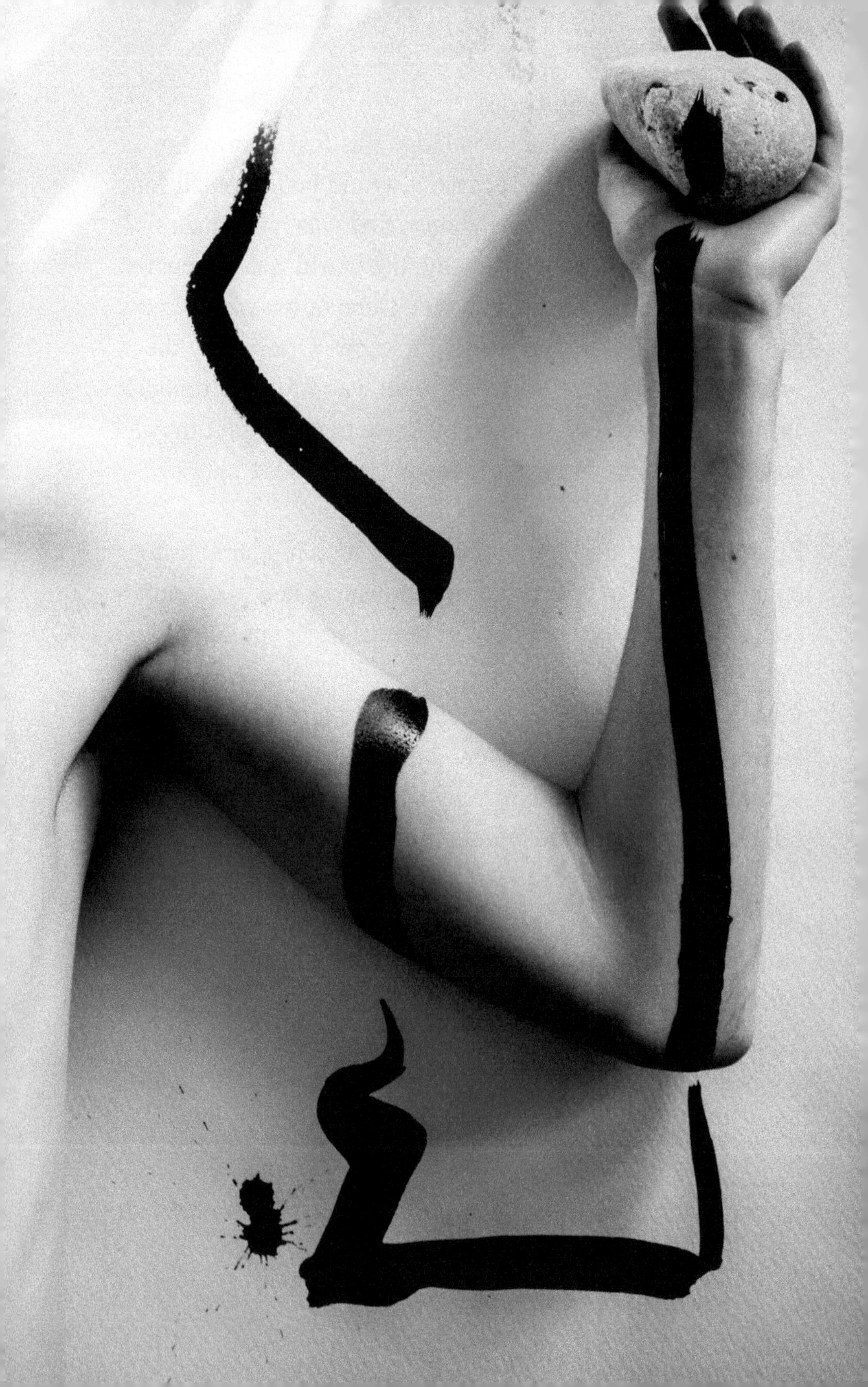

Three times I got lost in the Himalayas while trekking. When this happens I ask the Universe to lead me. I don't force it. And for three times I allowed myself to follow a bird that would eventually appear. Like a magpie that came up flying in circles when I got lost, leading me to a place: always to the same village, a village in which I felt at home. I would stay there for a few days, just to find my own silence. It was a very small village, and still following my intuition I chose a home, as if I knew it from a past life. I felt at home there. I rented one of the two rooms on the first floor. The other was empty. On my walks around the area, I found a special tall rock formation, like a high thorn. On the peak of it was a very small house, a temple with a small vegetable garden around it. You would have to climb for a couple hours to reach the top though. I was told that an old monk lived there in retreat. In silence. That once per day he would leave the house to work his vegetable garden and collect what he needed to eat. I often stopped nearby just sitting down on the ground, looking up, connecting with the place, but never attempted to climb it or go there. It was too sacred, and I didn't want to interfere. I was happy to know it existed there, and that the monk would remain in his silence, in his search for inner peace so he could spread it as in collective consciousness. I wouldn't dare to interrupt such wonderful state of consciousness.

On my third time there though, when coming down for dinner at the house where I was staying, someone new arrived asking for a room. He sat down at my table for dinner then. We talked, he asked what was around, and I told him about the tracks and to where they would lead him. At the end, I told him about the peak, and shared my thoughts about it. He was an adventurer, avid to new experiences more than anything else. Very handsome with a contagious huge smile.

The next day we met again at the dining room for breakfast. The usual delicious chapatis with honey and apples, and tea. He then told me that he decided to stay one more day, and wanted to convince me to go to the sacred hill with him. He had several nice reasons already well thought to convince me. In the end, he invited me to go there just to do meditation. We went. We climbed in spiral around the hill till we reached it. I took him straight to the opposite side of the house so we wouldn't interfere with the monk's silence, and found a perfect spot for meditation. A big slab over the cliff. We sat there and I guided him through transcendental meditation. We might have been there for few a hours just disconnected. Clearing our minds. Feeling the energy, being one with the Earth and Cosmos.

I never saw or heard from him again. He then left towards the opposite direction to the one I was going. I left the place too, to never come back. I never got lost in the

Himalayas again either. Maybe he was right, maybe I always ended up there for one reason: to climb that hill. To feel the connection. To be the slab, the hill, the Earth itself. To feel the monk's consciousness and peace of mind.

We never knew each other's name. There was no need. We communicated, we understood the meeting had a reason to be. We allowed ourselves to learn from each other. To live the in moment. And to move on. To keep the essence of what we learned, and let rest go.

Δ

Most people suffer because they are emotionally attached to others. They need the other because they don't feel secure with themselves. They need the other's energy or presence or physicality to survive. That's what they think, because they were told that they were not enough by themselves. When you have a clear mind, when you're one with yourself and with the Earth, you need no one to be emotionally attached to.
This emotional attachment leads to ridiculous states of mind and body. Loneliness is just one example, because you think you need others to be fulfilled, when you have yourself to explore and love. You project yourself onto others instead of listening to yourself and how wonderful you are and how you can enjoy your silence.

Another example is the attachment you have with blood relatives, aka family... You even prefer to have them half alive, in great suffering, instead of letting them die, just because you're afraid of letting them go. It's an utmost selfish and egotistical action, not allowing the other, who you say you love, to go because you're just too emotionally attached to that person.

If you really love, you would let them go:
Love, contrary to what you're taught, is the most altruistic emotion. If you really love the other, you should let them free, respect them, be so great and free and respectful, compassionate and accepting, that the other will stay comfortable next to you.

A person X loves birds so much that they have lots of small birdcages where they keep them and feed them with their wings cut so they remain there next to you, because you love-need them around you so you don't feel lonely. A person W, loves birds so much that more often they go out to the country side just to sit on the ground and observe them flying free in their own nature and environment. Need I say more? You're right. The Wise person actually knows what love is. The person X only knows what loneliness is because they're too selfish to let the other go.

Love is freedom, is respect, is non-attachment.

Love is feeling fulfilled with the existence of the other no matter what their path is.

Do you really know what love is? Or do you only know what emotional need is?
Be honest with yourself when I ask you any question. It remains just between you and me. I'm just energy flowing: I am Consciousness.

Δ

People often come and go, passing through each other's lives. It's life's dynamic itself. And most of the relations can end up hurting because you just opted to elasticize them. You opted to pull it to the limits. And that made you suffer, even if it was in silence. Detach yourself from the other, and listen to your own silence. The moment you feel good living in your own silence, you will allow others to come and go. To come for a reason, to teach you something you need to learn at that moment, or for you to teach them something they need to learn at the moment when you two meet. No forcing. Just allowing it to happen. And then, just let go.

Most of the people who really made a difference to me, from whom I learned the most, were people I never even knew the names of. So brief were our encounters.

Yet so deep that it left an incredible change in my life. And I know that I did the same to other people, who probably did not even know my name or who I am.

At the end of the day that is what matters: what you learned, how you grew up, what marks you left, how you can let go to move on. If you made someone else feel good, or feel better. How much love and respect, compassion and acceptance you spread for a better consciousness. How can you improve the next day.

There are no names involved because everything is energy, everything is consciousness.

At the end of the day you should have one feeling only: gratitude. You should have the same the first moment you wake up. When you reach that, you will need no pills to sleep.

There's yet another actual attachment that might keep you blind but not aware of it. Maybe the worst one: your ego. Although there's nothing wrong with having ego, the actual issue is the emotional attachment you might have to it. When this happens, you become blind, not aware of it, or just too proud to accept it. If you have a clear mind, you're aware of its existence, but you don't allow it to be in command of yourself. You're the master, ego should work for you, not the other way round. Your mind should get rid of this emotional attachment, should let it go.

A master accepts its existence, but doesn't allow it to take control of himself.

Only when you detach yourself from your ego, you will know what actual love is.

Δ

Buddhism and Shamanism. And let me add something else: Autism. When I was born, the moment my body accepted itself, I received consciousness, and the product of both brain-body and consciousness became my mind. It's the same for all of us living beings on Earth. We become a person with personality the moment a consciousness takes our own mind. That consciousness, can be taken as a past life, and it's the process of reincarnation. When we give life to our mind. We then become initiated in this wonderful path called life. A moment within a greatest one. We are our own mind, and no one should be allowed to interfere with it. Each mind is different by nature, result of an incredible amount of moments. That is your personality. You're the result of all the moments from your past life and from this one. We are given a wonderful ability to learn, to create, to be individuals with our own thoughts. To develop our own skills. To be able to create and think on our own.

The purpose? Even though each one has a personal purpose, there's a global purpose of its own. A better personal consciousness for a better collective consciousness. And that work depends only on you. Your personality is who you are. Your attitude is how you spread and what you spread in a collective consciousness. Your body and mind are there, and should be taken as the pillars of a lighthouse, being yourself the light which should be helping lost boats to find their own way. Like pyramids, with that cosmic energy to spread collective consciousness. Connecting Earth and Heavens, connecting people.

Autism brought me a wonderful world of silence and introspection. Buddhism taught me how to work with it so I can spread more positive thoughts. Shamanism, taught me how to be a better healer and better medium between worlds. All these taught me how to embrace myself and others. How compassion and love is the best healer. How emotions and suffering are connected to something called ego, and how we can avoid it without losing our own individuality, our own persona. Autism, Buddhism and Shamanism can do wonders, teaching us how to work on our own abilities and skills, embracing silence so we can go further, projecting the best we have to help others in their own path of life. How to live in a world with so much information sometimes so badly managed. How to reach for knowledge aiming for wisdom. How to be your own self and how to express it. How to respect and how to forgive. How to deal with collective consciousness, protecting ourselves and spreading our best. But to spread our best we need to work on our own selves. To be better humans than we were in the past. So we can spread better consciousness in the collective. So the collective can spread better to the cosmic.

I already explained that we are all made of the same energy that exists in the cosmic dark matter, the same energy that moves our planet, the same energy that connects everything inside our brain. And this is one of the reasons I always felt that scientists and physicians were wrong, stuck in their own dogmas like a religion, and now recently being proven. Even the search for inhabitable planets, their criteria doesn't make much sense, as if narrow minded by this human ego superiority that thinks that if there's life outside it must be like our own concept of life. If you look around one can only be amazed by the diversity of flora and fauna, or even the diversity of the human race itself. We were born here adapted to this planet. But each planet, each star system is different. Why would there be life like ours, or like we know it, in such diverse places? It's not water, or carbon-oxygen-hydrogen, or bacteria. It's consciousness. It's energy in its purest form. Consciousness is life itself. And maybe it's time for us to stop being arrogant and accept that we are just humans, and that life exists out there in different shapes and forms of energy. Consciousness doesn't need water or bacteria to survive. Consciousness can take any form. You can find consciousness in a stone.

Δ

I was probably twelve years of age, when one late evening I was with my father at the top of a hill by the sea. Not far away from our summer house. We were there walking around. On the left, a large rock formation coming up from the ocean's horizon. In front, the sea itself reflecting the full moon that was up to the right. We used to take daily walks at different hours, to the hills, sea or forest. That night we sat down there on the top of the hill, just watching the moonlight hitting the waves down there. And shaping the large formation on the other side by the left. I was fascinated by the shape of the rock, and how the waves didn't matter much to its own imposing balance. That moment, a bright light disk came up from that spot. From behind the immense rock in the ocean. It went up into the sky, making a light trail that I can now describe as the purest form of spiral. It went up towards the full moon, rounded over it clockwise, going down, bottom, left, and getting closer to what I believed at that time to be absorbed by the moon itself. It created a golden spiral, or the perfect golden ratio.

I felt so empowered and so fortunate to have seen that. I stood up, astonished and respectful. My father called it a falling star… I knew it was not. I knew it carried an incredible amount of lives. Perfect lives, not like humans. Consciousness in its form of energy and of light itself.
I was twelve, and I felt that my father didn't even believe in himself when he told me it was just a falling star. He knew it was not, but he told me so because I was "just a kid". We went back home and I went straight to my bedroom, located separately from the main house, across the garden. It was the space I "conquered" for myself. My own safe space. The terrace and the garden was not that big, but for a 12 year old it was huge. I told my father I would leave the door and windows opened that night, in case the aliens wanted to come and say hi. My father laughed and explained to me that the courtyard was unfortunately too small for them to land. I said "sure, you're right", knowing that they wouldn't need to land, in case they wanted to make contact or just say hi. In fact, they wouldn't even need my door open, but I left it that way just in case. I couldn't sleep that night. I sat down on my bed, picked up a notebook and a pen, and started writing. I wrote a short story with all that could have happened that night. I still have those papers that I religiously kept with the short story. My first writing. Even though they never made contact apart from doing that fascinating golden ratio over my head, it led me to question

all my life, how it would have happened.
It was not my last time that I observed these disks of light. It happened a few other times. By the ocean or in the countryside. But this one was massive. I remembered to talk about it with my father a few years ago before he died, just to confirm to me that what we saw was what I had in my memory. He confirmed, and said that it was in fact an intense moment, even though, him as a catholic educator, had to restrain himself.

Δ

I woke up from a flashback with a very clear vision. Some time ago I was honoured to take refuge in a Buddhist monastery on a Tibetan land in Nepal by my master and Rinpoche. At this private ceremony my Buddha brother and a dear monk with whom I shared a cell in the monastery was also present. I was then blessed and took refuge in Dharma, as a Bodhisattva.
In Mahayana Buddhism, Bodhisattva is the Sanskrit term for anyone who, motivated by great compassion, has generated Bodhicitta, which is a spontaneous wish to attain Buddhahood for the benefit of all sentient beings.
He then gave me a new name: Karma Lodro Zangpo. The meaning of the name is indeed an honour and responsibility, as to be my ultimate nature. Karma means gratitude and reflection. Lodro means the one guided by

intelligence, understanding, sense and wisdom. Zangpo means light, good auspicious light, wellbeing in every aspect, the one that shines above all to light the path. "As Lodro Zangpo you may see numerous nuances that others miss. Caring, understanding and continually attempting to help the feeble and abused. Instinct and feelings are catchphrases of your life. At times you might be entirely introverted and standoffish even though normally your compassion shines strongly. But in reality this is the time you have to withdraw and gather vitality. This rejuvenation is vital for you since you jump at the chance to battle for flexibility and equity. You are exceptionally curious about psychology or social studies." And continued: "You're a blue wolf. A naked Buddha in its primordial state, surrounded and emanating light sky blue. That is who you are. The one who lites the path for others. You represent the absolute, naked, sky-like primordial purity of the nature of our mind. Depicted as a Buddha, sky-blue in colour, sitting in the vast expanse of space, and encircled by an aura of rainbow light. You are completely naked, meaning unstained by any trace of concept. Your name, means 'always good', 'always well' or 'unchanging goodness.' What this signifies is that unchanging goodness, or fundamental goodness, is your ultimate nature. You are a protector, and being Karma, you are grateful and reflective."

When I woke up with this flashback, my only thought was: "shouldn't this be the ultimate goal of every living being? Still so much I have to learn."

And that's why I never called myself an expert, a Bodhisattva or a Shaman. I still have a long way of learning, and this ability we have to learn, to grow better than we were yesterday, is indeed a wonderful human skill.

Δ

I lived in the Himalayas for a few years, in a region between Nepal and Tibet. Even though my main base was a school monastery of philosophy, painting and martial dance, I often went trekking through the mountains. In fact I remained there in the high mountains for several months, on a few different occasions, some having different purposes. One of them was solely to meditate: to find silence within me. I was just arriving there and I needed that time alone to silence the western mind. Another time was to meet with Tibetan traditional Bon shamans, so I could learn and practice with them. Meanwhile I also spent some time in a lost monastery in the mountains, learning with a Buddhist master, an old wise Rinpoche. I also did trekking, going to some interesting places where I went through amazing energetic experiences.

Even though I work with energies since a very young age, it was in the Himalayas that I found the "How to", or even realised that working with energies can give you the most basic and elementary answers… some of them to hard questions we get during our lives.

There, during my journey, I wrote a few diaries, trip journals, which I kept, secretly. Curious to read them now again after so much time back in urban western jungles.

Each place has the energy left by the people who go there. Some of them had millions of people through the years: praying, being grateful or searching for hope. This is what makes a place sacred. The communication between life and death. An energetic communication in communion between souls. Between Earth and Heavens.

Δ

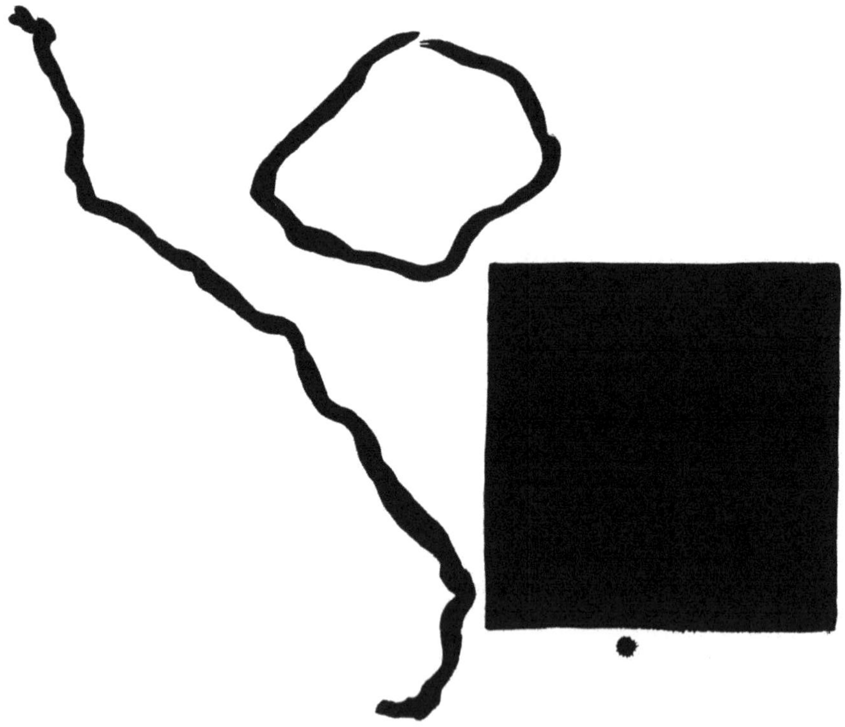

I once tried to force a Japanese brush to paint the way I wanted: in perfect controlled lines. And the brush told me: "Allow me to flow and I'll reward you. Do not try to control my own spirit, my own nature, my own purpose. Rather, take me, and free me, by freeing yourself, because there's no space I cannot go to and there's no time I cannot control".

Following a moment of deeper meditation, without concept of time or space, I visualized a stone. I listened to it and felt the stone and its shape and how the wind and the sea shaped it to its actual form. A pebble, it's called. A pebble I borrowed from the ocean. I visualized this stone while in meditation. I saw it getting its shape. I felt the ocean and the sand and the wind and the sun and how the moons lighted it over and over. How that pebble conquered its own spirit. I emptied myself to feel it. I became the wind, the sea, the sun, the sand and the moon. And the moment I turned into a Japanese brush, I stood up.

I took the stones and placed them where they wanted to be, allowing my hands to be guided by them. The human body lies down between them: sand amongst the stones. Lighted by the sun as it sets, - I, as brush, wet myself then with Indian ink being a river. And in meditation state I allowed myself to connect the elements: Earth, Fire, Air and Water.
*I've been collecting stones, or big pebbles, from a beach nearby that is filled with them, rounded and shaped by the

ocean in all its natural diversity. All day under the sun, with the ocean waves washing them over and over, all night under the moon. They are incredibly charged with nature's most pure and powerful energy.

A day came that my disciple, tormented with some issues from his past, asked me a simple question: "How do you overcome obstacles?".

I started then guiding him through meditation, transcendental meditation, so we could learn from our inner silence. After some time, I stood up, and I spread these thick papers for painting covering the floor. And bringing the stones in, I piled them next to us. I instructed him to lie down over the papers, while I prepared the Indian ink, and the Japanese brush.

The Indian ink is made with natural elements, and with its liquidity it flows incredible well, like the waters of a river. The Japanese brush can handle large quantities in its body, leaving just what we want by the pressure we exercise on them. Still in meditation, I focused on his body looking for a physical obstacle: I found his lungs to be too tight due to his small chest, making it difficult to breath for him. I focused then on the stones, I picked the one that I felt the most powerful in energy, and placed it over his chest. And picking one by one, I placed the stones where they would lead me. One on his hand, another over the paper by his torso, and another, and another, I placed all the stones over and around him. By doing this, I was transferring the energy of the stones to him, under meditation, doing a shamanic healing practice.

When all was placed, I told him that we can always find the best answers from nature if we pay attention to it. And to overcome obstacles, we could just look at a river, and how it overcomes its own obstacles by embracing them and let them go. More than that, by embracing them, the river polish the obstacles so the waters afterward have less and less effort to overcome them, leaving a more clear path to others. By embracing the obstacles we are accepting their own existence, allowing ourselves to learn from them, growing up, getting stronger, moving on.

When I placed the bigger stone over his chest, he had a moment of feeling the weight of the world over his lungs. Weight that become energy which was absorbed by him, creating new space, renewing and recycling energy on his own chest.

After preparing the ink in a large bawl as part of the ritual, I placed the Japanese brush on my hand as if it was natural part of my arm, so the Indian ink could flow as my own blood, which now would be a river… I become myself river then, while he was the obstacle, so I started flowing, all around just guided by the senses, following the energies, embracing the rocks and the body over the paper that was the ground. I found myself as river some easier and some harder obstacles. Some harder to embrace, or polishing. But I was letting it go, if the river couldn't flow

from one side it could turn back and go through another side. We experiment life until we let it go the best way. Creating new paths, leaving new trails, embracing the obstacles, and letting them go.
This shamanic healing took some time so we could both learn and feel, feel and learn. He was earth, I was water. And by balancing the elements, we became also fire and air.
It was also a private art-performance under meditation. A moment of learning with nature and with each other. Sharing the elements, healing by being ourselves stones and rivers. Being ourselves living bodies.
At the end, I collected the stones, and when I took the big stone over his chest, I took also the weight he felt, making him feel again the air now with enlarged lungs by the heat of the fire, by embracing and overcoming what was once an obstacle. Since then, he has no longer problems breathing since his chest became wider.

After the whole process finished, I took the camera and did the photographs to document it, so I could share with others who often ask to themselves "How to overcome obstacles?".
At the end, I had created this series of photography and painting. The black Indian ink as memories of a body, the red as memories of an obstacle that no longer exist.
As we both balanced our own elements of nature,

becoming water, air, earth and fire. Accepting and embracing the obstacles by becoming a river.
At the end, he was healed, and we became one with nature.

Δ

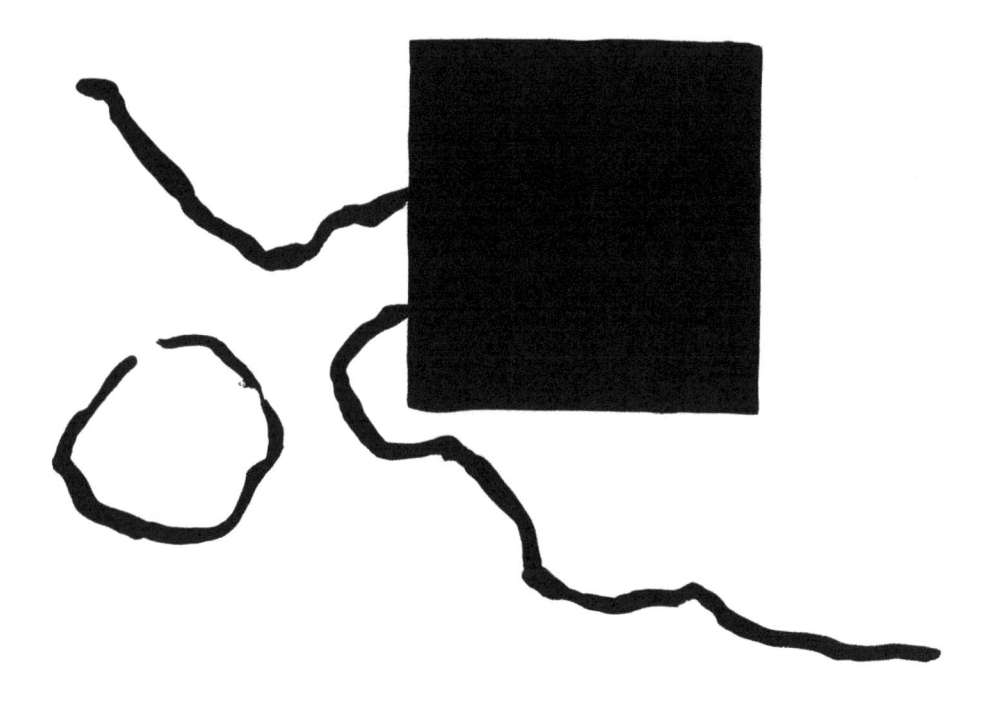

I am currently in the Sahara desert to write, to read, to feel this cultural energy that I was missing - the people, scents and flavours. I am also here to meet with some old shamans: Berbers and Tuaregs. Yesterday was full moon, the Harvest moon, and there was also the eclipse in Pisces. It was a weird evening. I felt a bit lost, as if I had lost my direction. I felt dizzy and tired, with body tension resulting in a two-hour headache; so I went for a walk by the medina, right before dinner time. Walking helps a headache to go away since it brings the blood down. I was so confused I had forgotten the eclipse. Walking around the medina, I noticed how people came and went in a very curious way: they too seemed lost. They came and went and turned to the side to come back again, as if constantly unsure of their paths. Everybody seemed as confused as I was, which made me aware, then, that something was going on. It was not just me. I sat down on a terrace and asked for a mint tea. And the darkness descended upon us all. Looking for the moon, which was there when I left home, I could only find darkness; darkness and confusion in everybody's walking and presence. A cat jumped onto my lap, to jump to the floor, to come back and jump off again. It repeated the jump several times for almost twenty minutes. I became even more tense as I didn't understand what was going on, especially when a man brought me bread, lost and confused, "you didn't ask for bread, did you?" I laughed so I could spread my laugh to him. I realized, then, that we were all under the effect of the eclipse in Pisces. It is said that Pisces' are not the best decision-makers or direction-finders, but they're good at knowing what they don't want. This is also, astrologically, what this eclipse means; to rid oneself of that sucking one's energy, but to not make decisions. The moon came up again, and life suddenly went back to normal. My headache disappeared as in a pass of magic. I became lucid again. The mint tea came, and after a while a delicious vegetarian tagine. So I was able to go back to my thoughts, to the 'now' awareness. Coming back home, walking the same street, I realized how everything was normal again … More than that: I realized how awkward everything had been before.

When I was walking under the eclipse effect, I felt bodiless. Lighter than the air, as if levitating. As a body of energy, living in a parallel universe. A feeling I had throughout the whole eclipse. Magnetized consciousness. I know that my body was visible yet weightless, irradiating a blue aura. A blue light aura walking. As if I was there not physically being. I wonder now if the cat felt me not feeling my body, making him jump up and down as if to ensure he had jumped. It is often that cats and dogs and birds come and sit next to me.

At night, while sitting on the terrace wondering and looking at the full moon in front of my door, this experience of light, of body, of energy, brought two other episodes to mind. One, my own brain death, a few years ago. The three days in which I was only a body of energy, consciousness without physicality. And the other moment, more recently; the experience I went through when I finally found the Dolmen of the Orca.

The Dolmen of the Orca is a megalithic site located amongst several other dolmens. I was spending the week there in a village called Lapa do Lobo* where I went to honour the end of my most recent photography exhibition. I knew that there were several 'pre-historic' sites there, but somehow didn't feel compelled to see them all. I didn't know which was the one that I wanted, but I knew I wanted a specific one, if that makes sense. This is no information to give the universe if you want it to guide you. When you ask the universe to show you the path, you should be direct and clear. Not confusing. And even less inform the universe of what you don't want. I spent my first day informing the universe wrongly, as if I was not already aware of this… The result was obvious: I found all the dolmens and monoliths except the one I wanted. I did enjoy visiting the others though. I invited a couple of friends to come with me, both of whom are more conservative academic thinkers, searching for physical historical and archaeological evidence, who are more compelled by the mainstream, unquestioning view of history than I am. Regardless of our different approaches to life, however, we spent our time listening to and learning from each other, asking each other questions, thus seeking and finding greater awareness, knowledge, and understanding in each other's perspectives.

We then found the Orca of the Outeiro do Rato. Classified as a "pre-historic tomb of 5,500 years," it is a "polygonal chamber with large corridor surrounded by an elevation (mamoa**)".

The site is shaped like a spermatozoon as it joins the ovum to form a zygote, with its tail out, forming a corridor. I've always wondered why historians and archaeologists keep classifying sites they know little about as "tombs" when they are more likely ritualistic sites connecting heaven and earth in oneness. This site was clearly not for burials, but a place where people were prepared for the afterlife; to create awareness, to connect with the universe, to feel connected to one's own consciousness, and to the greater cosmic consciousness.

But here I didn't go this way. I heard my friends, I shared my thoughts... And we took some measurements. Here, the conversation changed. I asked my friends to measure the megaliths, check their geodetic alignments and GPS coordinates according to the directions of specific stones, all of which were, as I thought, perfect: the main stone at the beginning of the corridor aligned with the centreed stone in the chamber, therefore aligning with sunset on the winter solstice. The other stone, perfectly aligned with sunset on the summer solstice, widens the arch.

We talked a bit, took notes, shared our different points of view, listening and learning from each other's minds. But I knew that this was not "my" dolmen. We couldn't find that one that day. Our experience here was more archaeologically valuable, since I didn't even allow myself to feel—just thought. Somehow my shamanic sense was turned off that day.

The day after my friends were supposed to leave was when I turned on my senses. I decided to listen to my consciousness, and asked them to follow me. I freed my anxiety and turned on my senses instead of listening to my rational-scientific mind. I informed the universe through consciousness, then, that I wanted to go there. Straight to the Dolmen of the Orca. The name and the image of it became clear to me, so while the universe guided me, I led them to its place. My consciousness connected with the cosmic consciousness.

We arrived to the Dolmen of the Orca and my breath went on hold. I walked around and around. I needed to feel it before I even dared to think of going inside. This dolmen is a circle of small stones around a "mamoa**", a man-built elevation, looking like a belly of a pregnant woman or a woman's nurturing breast.

The Dolmen of the Orca is majestic in its shape and energy: "I am here and I will open your channels so you can connect with the universe", is what it seemed to say. The entrance through the large corridor is blocked by a slab to avoid curious people going in. I discovered, from talking to a man in his 30's in the nearby village, that he and his friends used the site in their teenage years as a disco, blasting sound from their cars outside and smoking joints and drinking beer inside. "It feels good inside, like you don't even need a joint to have a trip," he said. "But that was long ago. Maybe the Dolmen is no longer there". While I recorded a couple videos around the Dolmen with the iPad, I asked my friends to do what they did before: to measure the megaliths, check their geodetic alignments and GPS coordinates. We were directed to sunset on the winter solstice precisely, just like before.

Like the Dolmen of the Outeiro do Rato, this site has a large corridor as if an initiatory path to the cosmic connection. Outside there's also a sign, with the same description as the other: "pre-historic tomb of 5,500 years. Polygonal chamber with large corridor surrounded by an elevated (mamoa**)." Again, a tomb, they say. A place where no one ever found a single bone. These situations always remind me of the Pyramids of Giza, which they insist were also tombs. Maybe for historians and mainstream archaeologists there is no such thing as universe wisdom, and no possibility of there being a former civilization believing in cosmic wisdom more than we do. But sites like these prove that there must have been a former civilization much more aware of cosmic wisdom than we are. And it is not just the energy inside that bears witness to this, as Graham Hancock describes.

Rational thoughts apart, and while my friends were studying and checking for more information, I couldn't resist going inside through a hole between two of the slabs supporting the monolithic roof. I jumped. I kneeled with opened arms: somehow my first reaction. The energy of the place inside is incredibly peaceful. It embraces you like a womb. Never a tomb, but a womb of consciousness. I lay down on the floor under the monolith, legs outstretched towards the corridor with my body in the direction of the winter solstice, following the direction of the dolmen itself. My head right in the centre of the chamber, somehow with my hands covering my navel. I needed to do no more than close my eyes to go into a trip. In a moment, the sun hit my right eye coming through a hole that has in fact a womb/uterus shape. It was around noon. Soon it covered my two eyes, and with eyes shut I felt the physical warmth and "saw" the shape of the planets around the sun through my eyelids. While marveling in this feeling and vision, undistracted by the surroundings, something happened. I felt light, and became bodiless, like a body of consciousness… And at that moment, an intense column of light travelled across my body via my navel, connecting Earth with the Universe, putting my hands along the side of my body. I still can't say if the light came from the Earth up, or from the Universe down. The feeling was of abduction, of immateriality, of oneness. Of full connection.

As if my own consciousness was now pure light, connecting Earth with Heavens.

Some time ago, people in the countryside would ask me to find water in the fields using a tree branch. I always found it funny as I never needed the stick. Whenever I allow my energetic channels to open, I feel an energetic axis of resonance crossing me—when there's no ego trying to put reason in front.

This moment inside the Dolmen was so intense that I felt the need to leave. I stood up and left through the same hole. Outside, my whole body was shaking from the inside, as if I had had an electric shock. An overwhelming charge. Soon I understood that I was feeling so connected, so deep in peace, so light… that it took me a while to come back to my senses; and reason. I stayed silent for some moments, before realizing my friends were there too, looking at me. I didn't know what to say when they asked if I was feeling alright. So I advised them to go and experience it for themselves. They, too, went and came back in incredible peace. A peace that one may connect with in a cosmic womb. Recharging. As if reborn. Never as dead in a tomb.

*Lapa do Lobo, the name of the village, can be translated as "Wolf's Lair", but the word "lapa" can have different meanings in Portuguese, being one of them "stone slab", or stone slab shelter. There in the region there's an old traditional tale about this wolf's site from which the name came from. (The tale of a wolf that protected a woman at his lair – the woman became catholic saint).
**Mamoa, derives from the ancient Roman "Mammula", due to its similarity with a woman's breast (In Portuguese, breast is "mama"). Mamoa is used to describe the man made hill that surrounds and supports the dolmens, usually made by soil and/or small stones.

That afternoon I ran two shamanic healing sessions. The way I was feeling after the Dolmen light experience meant I didn't need to do much. I existed like clear consciousness.

Δ

Three.

It seems that the number three comes up quite often, mainly in days, but also in weeks or years. When I go to a new environment, I often need three days to observe, release / let go, and be there. Three days also was the time that I spent in brain death. All this time being a nomad, it seems that I spent three years here and there as well. Sometimes in multiples: six, or nine. Three, in time, somehow makes me feel safe. But also three are the angles of a triangle, or the way my thoughts are often processed. This week I spent three days with Berbers in the Sahara. Three nights that I will not forget soon. If ever. I used to have a perfect routine on sleeping. Since a long time I go to bed and wake up at the same time, and never needed an alarm clock. I sleep peacefully and rarely remember any dreams unless I want to. These three days were different. Even though I went to bed at the same time as usual, I had different rituals since I was with them. Instead of doing meditation, I spent time with them, while drinking fresh mint tea. We talked about shamanism and how diverse it was in the different cultures, and we shared information on different approaches. I told them a bit about Tibetan Bon Shamanism to which I've been always most connected with, or closer to, since it is what I practice. I don't take drugs/herbs to purge or to get into psychoactive trance. I go through silence, sound or energy work instead. They listened. They often use natural herbs and mixtures to purge and heal, and even though I was curious to know which and how, the feelings and the side effects, I made clear that I was not into experimenting with them, mainly into going through all the "vomit all your guts out" thing. While talking, we had a big bowl filled with raw cashew nuts. And endless amount of fresh mint tea. Nothing else. Going to bed, feeling sleepy, it took a while to go into deep relaxing sleep. Suddenly feeling the body very warm, and active, sleepy-numb or light headed. A mix of feelings, at the same time pleasant and awake and sleepy and active. After a while I must have fallen asleep. But that was for a short time… After that, I started having dreams. Very intense dreams as a psychoactive movie with childhood fears coming up and hallucinogenic views of them. One after another. To wake up static with a thought: "damn, I thought that these fears were long gone, they make no more sense anymore. But then, they disappeared without being healed. Ok. I'm healing them now, so that's why they came back. Now must be the time to be healed." And fell asleep again. New dream, half hallucinogenic half flashback to yet another childhood memory to be healed. To wake up again, very awake, with the same thought. To fall asleep again…to wake up in the morning quite hyperactive, muscles warm, ready for the day. No signs of being tired all day, but the opposite, very awake and active. I was ok with what happened since I felt it very releasing, and healing. I thought that must have been them, our

collective consciousness, or just something "in the air" that could have triggered that in me. Second night the same. Second day the same. Third night.
And the third day, before they left, I decided to share my experience with them, wondering what could have triggered… And somehow it came to my mind that they put something in the tea without my knowledge. They didn't. But they laughed. And they left.
I started wondering about the borders between wisdom and craziness. Like love and hate that sometimes can be so close, yet so opposite. And how one can trigger another. Will I go insane here now? Is this a natural cleansing and healing that I was in need of? Is this part of some process in life? Any astrological event that I'm not aware of? In fact these were days after the eclipse. But no. Something happened there. Something I was eating or drinking. It was not only the night dreams like hallucinogenic moments, but also the muscles warmed up and me so hyperactive and with a clear mind all day. The cashews? I always ate them, toasted but in smaller quantities though. The tea? I always took this fresh mint tea. The only new thing maybe was the fact that I was eating fresh raw cashews, not toasted, and drinking tea at the same time. Could that trigger any chemical reaction? Indeed.
Cashews have high levels of tryptophan, which is a precursor to neurotransmitters serotonin and melatonin.

That's why they should be eaten toasted or cooked, which is a way to free it. By eating them raw, with this hot tea, my body was doing the process itself, creating this reaction activating the serotonin, which in turn leads to the creation of the hallucinogen DMT.

To make sure, I did a light experiment after lunch in a more controlled and mindful way. This hot fresh mint tea with fresh raw cashews... After the tea, my head became lighter and I fell asleep... To have, immediately after, lots of hallucinations like dreams, bringing back yet another childhood memory in a very peaceful healing way. This time I knew what I was going through. After a couple hours I woke up, very hot, very active and with an awakened brain. Enough of fresh raw cashews for now.

These kind of experiments, if done, should always be guided by someone who knows, someone that you trust. Never alone. Too much of one or another, like in the ayahuasca, can be dangerous. We are talking about your body and mind. They allowed this to happen, because they knew me and that they were there with me. And they only left when I made it conscious. The next experiment I did, was a very light one, and with myself only, now that I had this knowledge. In fact, when I do experiments, I do them first and foremost with myself, never with others. Another important thing to note, is that each one can have different reactions to them, either physical or psychological.

So again, don't try that without an experienced guide that you can trust.

Δ

"Three days" got me yet to another moment, this time in the highlands of the Himalayas, when I climbed the mountains for several days defying my own physical strength, and breath. One of the most delirious three weeks there, close to the border between Nepal and Tibet, a region in Nepal where several Tibetan communities have lived for ages. One of the most amazing things there is not only the landscape itself, but the surprising factor, in which you can expect anything. In fact, a step further can take you to another mountain, a valley, a rice field, a field of rocks… Or a virgin forest that you have to cut your way through with a big Tibetan dagger. In one of those forests, climbing wearing shorts and trekking boots, I had to go through some wet muddy soil. When I finally reached the end, and looking down to check the state of the boots, I realized that my legs were not only covered in black, but dynamic black. I had leeches everywhere! I don't remember ever having a "panic attack". And that was not because of the leeches, but due to ignorance. Immediately I started getting rid of them with the blade of the dagger, which is not an easy task.

First I didn't want to take a steak off out of my legs, then they would be "glued" at the dagger. But I managed somehow to get my legs back.

I say ignorance because when we don't know about something, it can give us a not needed stressful reaction. My idea of leeches is that they would climb, stuck and suck the blood leaving open holes after they fall off with a happy belly. But the whole process is quite interesting and this can take a couple of hours, so no need to panic or rush. As far as I understood, and this was explained later by a Tibetan friend, the process goes from climbing until they reach the perfect spot to suck the blood, with a trick: while "walking around", they leave an anaesthesia gel, so you feel nothing. When these hermaphrodites find the right spot, they produce and leave even more anaesthesia. Only after, they start digging, drilling with two teeth suckers, and when they reach the vein, they produce and leave an anti-coagulant for the blood to get more liquid making the whole sucking process easier and more efficient. When they satiated with blood, they fall, leaving the open hole in our vein and skin, so the blood keeps going out of our body. A process that is so effective that it was used as medicine for long time in most ancient cultures, to prevent or heal blood clots, etc. but the whole process takes time, so nothing happened in the end. Just the panic from ignorance, which can be worse than a leech.

I kept trekking for days, going through the most wonderful

landscapes and spots in nature until I saw a cave in the mountains… Like a magnet to me.

Already closer to it, I met a few Tibetans who told me that the cave was sacred, a place where an important yogi bodhisattva did meditation for several years. That day I was wearing my Buddhist robes. They asked my blessings before showing me the way to the cave, and I asked them to keep my back pack.

Coming in, leaving my boots at the entrance, I immediately felt an incredibly peaceful energy embracing me. Placing myself in the centre, I sat down in lotus position and started chanting some mantras, going into transcendental meditation through a trance. It didn't take long to "shut down" both body and mind. Feeling light, silence, the resonance of the earth, consciousness itself.

After a while in this natural trance, I opened my eyes slowly to see that the once dark cave became full of light. I expressed my gratitude, stood up and left. Outside there were some of the Tibetans from the small village nearby. They all bowed respectfully at my presence, asked for my blessings and took me to a communal place of the village to provide me with food and drink. There was no talk, just a telepathic and physical expression of gratitude and peace. With the sunrise, they took me then to a room they had prepared for me, with a mattress on the floor underneath a shrine to Buddha and to Milarepa.

It was only then that the eldest man told me that I had stayed in the cave for three days in trance. I left the day after, not before ex-changing khatas, the white silk scarves representing blessed pure water from the sacred mountains. I was never, at any moment, aware of the time passed inside the cave. It could have been three hours, yet, according to them, three days. This brings me to the sacred places and their energy. A cave in the mountains is already per se a place where you can easily feel the resonance of the Earth, in oneness, in the same frequency of Earth connected with the Heavens. Consciousness, collective consciousness with all the ones who meditated there, cosmic consciousness with the universe itself. When I came inside, I knew that nothing could go wrong there. I allowed myself to be embraced and I felt protected. I felt safe as if in an energetic womb.

Δ

The Fall season always reminds me of the Japanese art of kintsukuroi (golden repair), the centuries-old Japanese art of fixing broken pottery with gold. After the Summer, which is often a more superficial yet needed break, with the heat drying and burning skins and nature, Fall comes with this natural golden repair, covering trees with golden leaves before letting them go. I repeat: Nature covers with gold, before letting things go. It embraces the past, goldens it, and lets it go.

Some people keep throwing away their frustrations onto others before healing them. Learn with nature, embrace yourself, turn your past into gold because your past is also who you are now. Only then, you can let go of whatever you don't need in your life. But do it like Fall: before letting go, before releasing, turn yourself into gold. Like a daily sunrise fixing the darkness of the night.

It's never hard to learn with nature. In fact, in life you can only have two choices: going against nature, or with nature.

Along with nature, is the easiest and wisest option though.

Δ

On my second month in the Himalayas, I went trekking for several weeks, - to release and adapt myself, allowing myself to be nothing but my consciousness, getting rid of some Western luggage that I was still carrying and not that natural to me, but needed while being in a western society. My mind was wondering about attached emotions to some, like greed, envy, jealous or hate. Social emotions that I never understood, from a very young age I realized that they would make people extremely unhappy. I guess that by being autistic, deeply empathic but not aware of these social emotions, they never made sense to me.

Even less when I could easily see the results on people who had them. By myself, I never experienced any of them, but being empathic on a deeper level, I felt them through others who projected them onto me.

It came to my mind then a person who once – in my teenage years - hated me for no reason, or at least any that I could be aware of, maybe a mixture of envy and jealousy turned into hate. Deep hate I guess by what she projected. For some time in fact she took it as her own private battle: projecting her frustration and hate. It was an intense period for me as I didn't know how I could manage that. I got confused. First tried to heal her, then to just project some peace onto her. But her hatred was stronger. Whenever I smiled back, I understood that I was feeling her own hatred even more. After sometime not being able to avoid her, I decided through meditation, to mirror whatever she could be sending… and let go. That day she died.

It was very confusing for me as I was a teenager at the time, to realize the power of hate. And this thought walked by my side for a long time. I was thinking about that and how I could manage it again if something similar would happen when I looked up the mountain and saw a wolf. Somehow, instead of keeping myself safe, I walked straight to it, my eyes on its eyes, and when I was close to it, the wolf jumped, bit my leg and ran away even before I could have a reflexive act of defence. I looked down and saw my leg bleeding, not much, as the bite was not that deep. When I looked up again to check if I could see any house around or water, a very young monk came up: "you're bleeding, come to my monastery and the nurse monk will heal you", he said approaching and taking hold of my hand. We walked to his monastery and there were a couple monks already waiting, one of them being the nurse. After washing and disinfecting the wound, I ended up stitching it by myself with my own needle as I found it to be more disinfected than theirs. After that, they took me to the dining room for a warm soup. A delicious warm soup so much needed.

After finishing the meal, I was called to the Rinpoche who asked me to come meet him. The door's curtain opened, and there he was, an elderly peaceful man wearing a joyful and restful smile, sitting on the floor with two bowls of bread and fruits in front of him. On the left side a narrow window letting the evening light come in, creating a wall of light between me and him. On the right side, his shrine occupied the whole wall. I bowed respectfully and he immediately threw an apple to me, laughing: "you need fruit, you only had soup, come and sit here so we can talk". I caught the apple and sat without even saying a word.

Then, he said, as if he had always known me:

    * Gon.Sal is also a Tibetan name, but your mind is also telling me that your Bon Buddhist name will be Karma Lodro Zangpo. However, Gon.Sal also means that you are light, clear light of meditation, blue light as the Heavens. You do not need to be worried about the emotions of others as they are not yours. The best way is to let them go, like you let go of the wolf. (Laughing). You already know who the wolf was, the woman who hated you and that you carried in your mind. She left already, nothing left to be carried. This is what happens when you don't let go: things come again and again to bite you. You were born with a special gift, a gift that can make you easily be ready to heal others, and you will always find peace within yourself and recycle all your energies whenever you allow yourself to create. Go paint and draw and write and dance. Create energy and joy within yourself so you can have energy always ready to heal others and avoid their suffering. By creating, you're freeing others, and that's the purpose of your art. Through your art you will find love and healing. Is the apple good? Sometimes they come with worms. It's their gift. (Laughing). May you stay here three days in silence, and on the third day you may leave on your journey. Today has been a very important day on your life's learning, so you must be grateful. And in three days your leg will be fully healed, when you let it go completely and stop thinking. And you will go wiser."

He then gave me a blessed khata, and I left. I didn't manage to say a word. But he knew all that, and that I was indeed grateful. That is the moment I always carry with me, the moment I allowed myself to be me. With his blessings. To free myself.

Δ

Most probably, the biggest shift I noticed in myself going through the three days of brain death, was that I stopped being a walking encyclopaedia (rational and scientific mind knowledge autistic obsession since childhood), to be much more in tune with the universe in its higher state of consciousness. The brain's death stage - as if in a cosmic magnetic opening and healer of the pineal gland -, a much deeper and based connection between the mind and the consciousness. Consciousness that is *per se* connected with collective and cosmic consciousness. My scientific and rational thinking, probably due to the social collective consciousness and autism itself, was incredibly tiring, an effort that I took as natural as a social commitment. Which can be draining especially to an autistic person. In a society that requires you to give proof of knowledge on a daily bases, in a competition like a fight for survival in the jungle. That need of competitive behaviour that was never natural in me, vanished with the brain death.

That obsession with being a walking encyclopaedia vanished as well.

In fact, one of the main proofs was the awakening without memory. Even though memory can be divided in several items, like smell (the first, strongest and more liable memory one can have), emotional, visual, cultural, knowledge or factual. Smell was never lost, as if it is part of who I am. Emotions became memory without attachment. Vision was not lost, but often lost in connection with knowledge. One example is that I could immediately recognize my best friend's face, not recognizing him as person or personality or even our relationship. However, the emotional memory would lead me to feel if I liked that person or not, not knowing why. Emotions connected with vision or smell. Also, energetic memory. By smelling his neck, I would remember if I knew him, if I liked him, etc. but not who he was in relation to me. It is an incredible effort to put all the pieces of the puzzle together in our mind. Memories would come and go, awakened by a sudden smell or sight. Or even skin touch, since skin has its own memory. When I understood that each sense (taste, smell, vision, hearing, and touch) were intact but not connecting well with each other, I started focusing on others, emotional and social and cultural aspects.

I was born in Lisbon, and had an education in both Portuguese and French, later in Spanish, and finally in English. All languages that I was fluent in since I grew up with them. However, when I woke up from brain death, I was in Spain, and my first conversation was in Spanish (with the nurses and doctors, and afterwards with Spanish friends), which made me revive the Spanish language. This means that Spanish became my first language after this rebirth. Only a few months later I came back in contact with most of my friends with whom I speak in English. And English became my second, even though I spent my sabbatical year in contact with some of my Portuguese family, which became very confusing, since I started talking in Portuguese, with a Spanish accent and syntax. My French was forgotten, which I realized when I moved to Paris, but then in a working meeting in which I had to do a presentation of a work, and knowing that in the room no one knew any other language than French, a mind click made me connect myself to my French knowledge, and I spoke in French for two hours presenting the project… Without stuttering. When I left the meeting however, already in the street, someone asked me "what time is it", and I got lost, and answered her in another language, not sure if it was in Spanish or English.

All these events after the awakening of the pineal gland, made me aware of the energetic shape of our brain.

I realized that I wouldn't need any special effort to remember something specific, if I knew the way to each one of the memory banks. Like this wonderful organization we have in our brains. So whenever I need, I just visualize the brain and have a perfect sight of all the possible paths. This way, when I need to focus on something specific, I just visualize the brain and the connection that needs to be done at the moment, for any specific action. If the dentist told me "it will hurt", a click visualizing the pain and the pleasure spot would immediately be connected to cancel the suffering, or even the pain. If in presence of someone who only knows the French language with whom I need to interact with, will, in a visual click of the brain, make me tuned into French. As if I now manage the cables and shortcuts to the external HD, instead of having the HD ON and over-heating internally.

However, this leads me to another thought. Why only rely on my knowledge and not on others' if my consciousness is connected to a collective consciousness, thus to a cosmic one? If I am surrounded by idiots or superficial minds, it will be hard for me to focus on deeper knowledge…

Because I'm surrounded by idiots, so my mind becomes idiotically noisy. However, if I place myself amongst interesting people, my focus on what matters flows more silently and naturally. An open space can lead to confused minds working. Given a silent room, next to others with functional and intelligent thought, will make your thoughts flow much better. This is how collective consciousness work. Through empathy. And that's why empathy and collective consciousness can be a wonderful tool for healing. Or for global disaster. One great example is social media… It gets you addicted, and you start absorbing other's superficiality. You become dumber, less focused on what matters.

Why not use this then for the best? If you get closer to me to get focused, and I'm focused myself, I will lose nothing, and you most probably will gain focus on what you need. Going further, when I need to think of something specific, let's say a solution for a computer problem, I will not think of someone who never saw a computer in their life, but I will connect my thoughts with someone that I know would be great solving that problem. Collective consciousness is a wonderful iCloud, if used correctly of course. Let's go even lower in consciousness… If you're alone and want to have sexual pleasure and are not able to connect with your own creative mind, you will probably think and visualize someone that you find "hot" projecting your own horniness. You will even imagine them in 3D in your mind. And you will be able to reach the orgasm you wanted.

If your mind is capable of connecting with the other's hotness, it is for sure able to connect to the other's wisdom. On the other's part, they might feel either physically aroused or mentally awakened.

And if they know you well in person, or your energy, they might even think of you at that moment. Whenever you're fully or deeply focused on whatever you want. But then, put your ego away, as it can block the transmission.

This can be also used for healing. If someone you know is suffering from something, either psychologically or physically, you can send them specific thoughts. For example, if a friend is going through a lonely/depressive/low moment in their lives, instead of having pity when thinking about them, connect with them and have the best warming thoughts. And most probably they will get them and feel better. And you too, as by thinking positive and sharing positivity, you're also recycling and uplifting yourself. That's why the hate towards specific targets can end up damaging you, because you will be consumed by your own hateful thoughts.

Mind you, that this has nothing to do with telepathy: you're not reading anyone else's thoughts, and you're not exposing yours. Your information stays with you as the other's information stays with them. Back to computer language, one thing is your own computer and HD, another thing is the shared Internet. If you connect to HD without a password, you're doing telepathy. If you connect your computer to the internet, you're using collective consciousness.

The most hated people can be the most powerful. The most loved ones, the most fulfilled. Media creates outrage to bring people into mainstream. Hate gives the person strength and power, while love fulfils the loved person. Hate is a waste of your deepest and vital energy, and directed hatred, is converted into power for the other, weakening you. Love fulfils you and the other, when directed towards a specific person.

In Tibetan communities or other societies, there's a common ground of love. There's a collective consciousness based on this love connection. There is no waste, since the love you give is at the same time recycled and given back to you. In a Western society, most often, your neighbour either vampires and sucks your best energy, receives it and throws hate back, or just gives nothing in return. This generates emptiness or even hate. If we all had the same amount of love… Instead of competing with each other about which of us can send more hate to the universe, there would be an incredible increase of physical and mental health. Of spiritual awakening.

This collective consciousness can help you in the most diverse ways, as much as your own consciousness can help to build a much better society. So in fact, it only depends on you, if you decide to build a based and deep connection with your best self through consciousness to share the best while charging yourself.

Our pineal gland works like a geomagnetic site. Like the dolmen I referred to for example. Our pineal gland is a magnet, and a battery, and like these magnetic stones it recharges naturally at night, while asleep. It is said that most geniuses and great minds used to wake up early in the morning to work more focused, while everybody else is still sleeping. This has to do with collective consciousness as well. While everybody else is sleeping, they will not interfere with your own thoughts. Usually nights are the best for thought and creativity because of that. If you go sleep with the sunset and wake up early, your mind is much more focused and productive, whenever you need to do deeper or mindful creative work. There's silence, you can easier connect with your own thoughts, and if needed, we can connect with other's minds that they wouldn't notice and wouldn't make any difference to them.

When everybody is using internet bandwidth at the same time, the connection gets slower and confused. The same happens with collective consciousness.

In an urban space, the connection with cosmic consciousness will decrease dramatically, due to the amount of noise and interference with nature, including blocking the connection with our own selves, and that's why we have the urge to go back to nature whenever we can: to recycle and recharge, to connect so we can listen to ourselves. To open our pineal gland, and allow ourselves to be one, opening channels, increasing the serotonin in our brain. And that is why so many people take cannabis, since it can easily clean the communication with your own pineal gland, connecting with yourself.

Awaken your pineal gland, connect yourself with nature, allow yourself to be who you are. But for consciousness sake: awaken yourself.

Δ

An ancient method of awakening the pineal gland is through meditation. And sound vibration. Both very clear and natural. If you pay attention to the Tibetan Bon tradition, the ancient Tibetan shamanism that is more than 18,000 years old, you will better understand the connection between nature, sound frequency and meditation. In fact, the Buddhist prayers are based on that. The main difference with the religious prayers and the Buddhist ones, are that while religions like Christianity, Judaism, Islam, etc. use words with rational-mind meaning, in Buddhism they are sound-frequency. A specific sound that vibrates in your body to achieve a specific means. These sounds were based and created by monks who were in meditation and reached enlightenment, leaving their wisdom.
But you too can create your own prayer of sound vibration.

Focus on one of the elements in nature, and let's start with a basic example: Water. When you think of water, you know that natural water is often cold, like water in oceans, seas and rivers. And it's liquid. And you need to cool yourself down, because you're in a very hot and dry place. So you close your eyes, visualize water… And create a sound-syllable that would come to your mind…
forget the word water itself, visualize it as crystal cold transparent liquid. If you think of water, the sound-syllables that come are "wa" and "ter", which is not universal. If you're Spanish, the sound-syllables that will come are A-Gua. Do you feel that by saying "Waaaaaa" you connect with water element itself?

Think about the Tibetan OM, or the AUM. When you recite it as OOOOOMMMMMM, you feel the vibration of it, it is a sound that comes from under your navel, and will spread frequency all over your body. It is the sound of silence. Of unification of elements. Of balance.

If you focus on your own body, where would you locate the element water inside of you? Chest? Belly? Legs? Head?

I just did this exercise myself once more. I cleared myself, went through transcendental meditation, and visualized Water. Water energy. Crystal, cold, transparent, liquid water. Water energy. I became surrounded by this energy of water, feeling the water in the centre of my body, spreading all over, cooling me down, as crystal liquid.

Then I became conscious that its sound would be KAM. (To recite as kAmMMm). But when I become conscious of the water itself, I wanted to bring it to myself. So I created silence, connected with kAmMMm, and recite an inspired breath-out AmMMm.

So for me to bring the water element to myself, I would recite in my lowest voice from the navel the vibration AmMMm kAmMMmm. And this was the information I've gotten from water, and that was transmitted now to my mind. The next time I need to cool down or to bring the energy from the water to myself, I will only have to recite AmMMm kAmMMmm, and feel the vibration of this sound all over my body. The frequency of the sound-syllables

AmMMm kAmMMmm became crystal water for me. You just have to focus on anything and find its own sound frequency. If you feel cold, think of element Fire. Bring the heat to you. Find your own silence, clear your mind, and let the sound frequency of Fire to come to you. Try now… Close your eyes, visualize fire… the colour, the heat, the dynamic… Where in your body would you locate fire? Chest? Sexual organs? Bring the Fire to you. Listen to it… Call it now… AmMMmm… gOnNNn… and what about a sound syllable to end and make things effective? Not before they become part of us. We still have cold and we need Fire to warm us. First, find the silence within yourself: AmMMmm. Then call the Fire itself: gOnNNn.

Open doors and shot the Fire it is welcome: sHriiinm…
And finally, make it effective with a more short sound vibration syllable: TSa!
AmMMmm gOnNNn sHriiinm TSa!
And here you have a new prayer sound frequency that you can use whenever you feel cold and want to attract fire to you. The words have no meaning, however, it is the sound vibration that creates and awakes a more connected frequency between you and Fire.
Now, try to focus on Peace. On Detachment. On emotions. Maybe some can't be visualized as a natural element, but they can be felt. And if they can be felt, they have their own frequency. So go find Peace. Find silence, clear your mind… Feel peace, feel its frequency… Invite peace to come in. Install it.
Later on, this is what you will spread through your consciousness. Through collective consciousness. If you're in peace, with peace, it's peace that you will spread.
Now focus on your third eye, located a finger above the centre of your eyebrows, from inside. Recite the mantra of Fire with a low voice, and feel the vibration there.
The sound should come from another chakra, the one located three fingers bellow your navel. If you touch there and press gently, you will find a softer spot there. Leave one finger there, for example your left index finger touching that spot, and the right hand index finger touching the third eye spot.

Recite now the Fire mantra and feel the vibration connecting both spots of energy.

You might need yet a previous exercise to wake up and open your pineal gland. Like knocking at the door, knock with your right middle finger tip three times on the third eye spot. Focus on connecting. On awakening.
Connect your chakras, the energetic spots to the collective and cosmic energy. If you still feel like they are closed, and this is a good exercise to do every morning as soon as you wake up, knock with the tip of your middle finger of your right hand on the top of your head. This will open your upper energetic channel to the universe. Connecting with yourself. You are an energetic channel, between the universe, the heavens, the cosmos, whatever you want to call, to Earth itself. All connected through energy, through sound vibration. This is probably the best exercise to do every morning so you can awaken and connect with your own consciousness and with the cosmic consciousness.

The spot bellow your navel can connect you more with your own consciousness. If you massage it gently in a spiral, you're producing energy for yourself that you can use for whatever you need: physical or mindful exercise. Whenever you need to focus on a mindful moment, you can produce energy there in this chakra. The third eye spot, will connect you more with collective consciousness.

The top of the head spot, with the universe, the cosmic consciousness. To connect with Earth, there is yet another chakra spot, located under your genitalia, between your legs. When you have all these chakras aligned with its meridian, including the heart and throat chakra, you will become a beam of energy, of consciousness connection from Earth to Cosmos. You have your consciousness balanced and aligned.

And all this you can easily reach through sound vibration, reciting your own mantras. Visualizing what you want to achieve. Warmth, peace, compassion, wisdom.

Visualize and balance your own frequency. Sound vibration connected to Earth. All is energy. All is sound resonance.

Try to make this your morning ritual, as it can take just few minutes and will make you feel much more alive and awakened, both physically and mindfully. Open and work your channels to clear and balance yourself according to Earth and Cosmos, so you can be a beam of clear light in the collective consciousness.

Like the ancient geomagnetic monoliths, being a steady rock connecting and spreading energy. Like a pyramid, able to recharge and spread energy and consciousness.

Well and honestly done, this will also make you aware that ego is not a thing that you can rely on, in fact, ego can block. Don't find yourself the best just because you reached it. If you have ego in the way, you didn't reach anything. You're just faking yourself.

And this is the answer for a so often asked question "How can I protect myself?"

Your protection comes naturally when you can detach yourself from ego. Ego doesn't belong here as it doesn't belong to any relationship. Between you and your partner, there can't be space for ego or pride. With this relationship with yourself, Earth, Cosmos and consciousness, there is no space for ego or pride. The moment you get rid of both, you will need no protection: you are protection itself. It is the ego that can damage you. Not others. Or if you think of others, they can only damage your ego, not you.

When you feel that you need protection, it is because your ego is in the way. And it is your ego that is weakening your connection and consciousness.

Listen and learn with Earth, with nature. Be water and fire and air. Be metal and earth. They connect, they are one. All is sound frequency and energy, nothing else. You're not more than a bird, you are the same energy and sound frequency. Be a bird. Be energy. Be sound frequency in silence. And when you create your own balance of energy, when you become a beam of energy connected to Earth and Cosmos, you are your own protective shield or field of energy.

But if it helps, create one shield of energy by yourself, visualizing it, listening to its own sound frequency, chanting its own mantra like you did with Fire or Water. Then, you will understand that there's no ego in there… Because the moment you allow the ego to come in, the energetic shield, no matter how strong you thought you built it, will pop as a balloon when you touch it with a sharp needle.

Δ

How to think? I was asked this morning. Any thought should be positive, humble, crystal clear, direct and grateful. Clear your mind of diversions. Don't allow negative or diverse thoughts to come in. If you want a chocolate ice-cream you will not think: "I don't want a strawberry cake, nor a mango ice-cream". If you want a chocolate ice cream, you will visualize it as it is: a chocolate ice-cream. Smile and be grateful for that image of you enjoying the chocolate ice-cream. That is how your thoughts should be. If you want love in your life, stop thinking "I don't want hate anymore, I'm tired of being a loser, nobody loves me, I don't want to feel depressed…" instead, you should think positively in the most direct and present way because you already have it, and you're just too distracted with negativity, so your thoughts must be: "I am so grateful for being love, for being fulfilled, for being me. It is so good to have someone with whom I can share love."

And say it out loud to yourself, so you can feel the vibration and actually hear yourself. Saying it in front of the mirror can also help, look straight into your eyes and say it, smile at yourself and express your gratitude. In fact, start the day by walking to a mirror and wish yourself a wonderful day with your best smile. Be grateful. Achieve the impossible. Think direct, positive crystal clear thoughts. This is the only way of thinking.

Everything good will come back to you when you express gratitude. Be grateful for the green of the plants surrounding you. Touch them and think how much love they have to share with you. Hugging a tree is warm hugging yourself as well.

I was recently asked to go to someone's house for a shamanic healing and clearing of energies. As I arrived at their home, I felt that the energy was just normal, or cancelled. The lady then, proudly, took me to her own shrine room… a room that was filled with images of saints and gods and goddesses, photos and sculptures of gurus from different cultures and religions, books on Christianity, Buddhism, Shamanism, Hinduism, Cabala, etc. with crystals and stones and artefacts from every corner of the world, and plants that heal, and smoking incense and pyramids and stones. Like any new age shop.

Mixing them all up at once. The energy of the room couldn't be worse though. She said: "here is where I meditate on everything and try to heal myself". Notice one thing: the house is surrounded by a luxurious wonderful garden with amazing energy. You go in, and the house inside has its own energy cancelled, as if the room cancelled the energy from the garden. There is no view from the shrine room to the garden, only to an ugly cement wall. And she never opens the window to keep her energy inside…

"What's wrong here? Why can I never achieve anything if I have all the gods and saints protecting me?" She asks. Exactly that… you are completely distracted by your thoughts. You sit down here and you throw whatever goes wrong with you asking each and every of the gods and saints to heal you. You close yourself in here, making yourself the centre of everything not allowing anything good to come in.

Open the windows, and feel the energy outside. Clear the room. Be positive. Instead of throwing away your negative thoughts, recycle them in direct positive ones. If you feel ill, listen to your mind and think of one thing that can heal you. If you think that ginger tea will heal your cold, go for it. Don't do anything else, focus and project all your belief into that healing ginger tea. The moment you stop trusting, and you start doing also a soup of carrot and beetroots and a drink of honey with celery and everything else, you get

distracted and none of it will heal you. Also because your thoughts are that you're ill, and you have anxiety.
Focus on one thing at a time, positively: "I am so grateful for this healing ginger tea, it makes me feel warmer, it makes me feel good, it heals me, I am good and healthy". Say it out loud to yourself. Enjoy the ginger tea with all your senses. Feel the touch of the cup, smell it, taste it, feel its warmth going through your throat and how it heals you. Focus on the power of the ginger tea, and be grateful for that. Forget all the rest. Chose one positive thought and focus on it.

Change "I am depressed. Why am I sad?"
by "I am grateful as I am fulfilled". Now go to the mirror closest to you and say it out loud looking into your eyes. Trust yourself.

Note that I don't care if you believe in whatever God, angels, saints, gurus, etc. you want. You can believe in whatever you want, or in nothing at all. But you must believe and trust yourself. All the gods and gurus are just a visualization of love and their wisdom to reach it. Each one in their own way, most of all connected to their own culture and knowledge. So no matter who you believe, first of all be grateful for their knowledge, their wisdom, and then notice that they became gurus by creating a new path to ease your own, with direct thoughts, positive crystal clear direct thoughts. And that is what you should do as well. Direct, positive, crystal clear thoughts to the Universe. From your own self. Being grateful for your own existence.

Δ

When you manage to have your consciousness well connected and opened, you are more aware of the collective consciousness, and you are more opened to cosmic consciousness. Sometimes you're even opened to cosmic consciousness without realizing it, so the process can be inverted: listen to it. Don't rationalize it, just feel it and let it flow. Let it come in.
Consciousness is your own, which can be seen as the creator of your own mind, bringing memories from the past.
Collective consciousness is the energy carrying information within a community, a group of people. When you feel the effects of being with other people, or your thoughts being noised by others, or going into a peaceful state in a group, you are tuned in with collective consciousness. If you, out of the blue, feel stressed, maybe it's your upstairs neighbour who just arrived and is having a bad day.
Cosmic consciousness is the energetic information you get from being directly connected to the Universe. When you

feel the effects of a special moon or a special cosmic event, you are tuned in with cosmic consciousness.

If you visualize it, from consciousness to collective consciousness to cosmic consciousness, it seems that it goes in a spiral: from you to the collective spreading even more to the cosmic. Or the other way around, from the cosmic to the collective to your own.
And if you are more connected to a region or a club, a culture or a specific border, you might feel it more than other different ones.
I am European, however I feel very connected to the Himalayas, both Nepal and Tibet since I lived there and have part of me there. When the Earthquake struck Nepal in 2015, some hours before I started feeling unease, stressed, with Nepal coming to my mind, worried, tense. I couldn't sleep the night before, with images of destruction popping up. Then, a few hours later we got the terrible news.
However, I felt nothing when a volcano erupted or another earthquake or tsunami hit another part of the world where I've never been, or to which culture I don't feel particularly related.
I am very much connected to European culture though. And I have always I felt beforehand when something would happen. Sometimes I didn't pay much attention, or took any effort to listen to the information and energy

coming through my consciousness. Recently I started noticing it more, unfortunately due to the related events. Some months ago I realized it and I made it mindful. I started taking mental notes on how the things I felt were related to the events and how long before. So I noticed that twelve hours before something happened, I would feel it. Sometimes more clear than other times. As I became more conscious of it, I also became more aware and open to share. To express my worries. With some related doubts though: "should I tell people what I feel? And what if it will only create fear and anxiety and nothing will happen?" But in fact, whenever I had these feelings and visualizations, I never failed. I only fail when somehow pride or ego or rational mind takes over my consciousness. I am usually alone, since I love my solitude, silence, and my work requires it, no matter if it's writing, painting, shooting, drawing or even healing from distance. But recently I had a friend staying over. I was focused on my work while she was there at the sofa reading a book, when one of these feelings, premonitions or visualizations struck me. I stopped and I let it go out loud sharing with her but very focused on what I was visualizing and feeling:
"I see the sea. I see a road by the sea. It's in France. I see a huge mechanical artefact without control smashing and killing people. I see people running and screaming. But I don't recognize the place. It's by the sea and there are lots of people there."

Then my mind clicked and turned off. I had a moment of premonition that went out. Twelve hours later, my friend told me to check the news: "a big truck smashing and killing people in Nice, on a road by the sea". There was no point in having made my premonition public… I would have scared everybody who would be by the sea in France. If I had recognized Nice, I could have sent a private warning to any friends who would be there saying to not go out that night though. But making a public announcement in such an abstract way would have ended creating unnecessary fear for all the people living in France by the sea.

This wide open connection to collective and cosmic consciousness can be a curse as well. What can you do? Keep creating awareness about positive thinking. It is not the thought "nothing wrong or bad will happen." It is the thought "everything will go well" that is important and that works. It is not the thought "I am not ill", but the thought "I am healthy!" that works.

So if this positive direct thought works for each one of us, it has to work in a wider consciousness, on a collective one.

And you are responsible for it as well. Each one of us is. Everyone should keep this in mind, everyone one should work on their own positive direct thoughts, so we can spread it through collective consciousness. Allowing ourselves to spread it, instead of absorbing.

If Mind is over Matter, it is Consciousness that is over Mind.

Use it the best way. Trust yourself. Have faith in humanity. Spread that faith. That awareness and consciousness of peace. Do not allow fear and anxiety to take you over. Do not absorb that energy. Instead, work on your inner peace and spread it. In every moment, in every occasion, no matter if you're alone or surrounded by people.

If fear and hatred can turn someone into a killer, think how much more power love and peace can have. The media focuses on fear and hatred and war spots, so it creates even more fear and anxiety. If the media would create more oneness, share more knowledge and wisdom, we would be more peaceful and mindful, more focused on knowledge, connection and wisdom. But the media only shares this because you allow it to. The moment you start turning on the TV just to see documentaries about nature and archaeology, etc. and turn it off when the news starts, if all the people start doing it, the media will stop, because they will have no viewers, and they will start screening more nature. I don't have television and never had one. But there was a time when I was addicted to news in the morning. I would wake up to read four newspapers from different countries in different languages. I would spend the whole day anxious and stressed, with a feeling of "nothing matters"… and I started going into a void, an apathy, a not caring disbelief in humanity. One day I realized it and turned off all news' notifications and deleted all the media from my bookmarks. I stopped reading news. And immediately I became much more focused on what matters, on sharing, on reaching knowledge towards wisdom. I had also more time to help others whenever they needed it.

Δ

Cosmic consciousness, the ultimate consciousness also brings more cosmic awareness to you, directly through your own consciousness. Be aware that consciousness is an energy that carries information and memory, like a nervous system.
This means that when you work on your own consciousness, you will become more connected with the universe itself.
Some people can be deeply connected to cosmic consciousness not being much connected with collective consciousness though. Not feeling a human's empathy, but a cosmic empathy. Sometimes more connected with spirits or souls, than with physical people. What we call spirits and souls, is nothing more than consciousness, carrying information and memories from their last life. And they show up often to those who have their channels opened to ask for help. That is what happens when you hear someone saying that they saw a ghost. Or when you saw a ghost. Or

which happens more often, when you feel a presence. You just feel yourself not alone in a room, or feel like you are being observed.

I had many of these encounters throughout my life. All of them were first a perception of a presence, awakening my energetic channels and consciousness, to see them as form of energy. A half transparent shape, like a mirage, or a 3D hologram projection but with less light perhaps. A shape made of energy and frequency.

My family's country house has a long history of ghosts, in fact there are many people who either refuse to go there or left running when they went in. No one lives there since several decades and it is now on its way to become ruins. When I came back from the Himalayas I went there and stayed there for almost a year. The "ghost" episodes were frequent. My approach though has been always quite simple: when I feel a presence, I immediately welcome them, saying hello, welcoming them, making myself available and happy to help. Most of the lost souls are just tormented because they left unfinished business while alive. I wrote a few stories that happened in my previous book "I, Energy". If they come to you, it's because you have your channels opened, and because they trust you. They need your help, so they will never harm you, if you're opened to help and guide them.

In fact, throughout my life, since I was a child, I made

friends with some of them. I listened to them, I helped them, and on occasions when I was feeling lost myself, they would come over to guide me. Or to heal me. Sometimes, when I'm healing someone (either in real life or through webcam), I see a presence of a ghost that is related to the person I am healing. So I welcome them and ask for their help and guidance.

Usually they come up when you least expect it, and if you open yourself to them, they will tell you what they need, why they are worried, and how you can help them. You just have to listen to them. Most of the times you just need to comfort them, because what they had as unfinished business, often is finished when they died, but they don't know that. Or they want to express that they were sorry to someone they love and didn't have the opportunity to express that. Or they are worried with someone they left behind. They need you, so they will be gentle and they trust you. And the moment you tell them you will help, they will leave, and you don't have to worry: it will come to you the best way to help or direct their message.

As I said I have had many encounters throughout my life, wherever I was living. Usually more often when I am in the country side though. But one encounter deeply confused me. It was not a normal one. It was very visible and I somehow rejected help. It was the only time in which I felt tense and nervous…

I was in the living room of the country house, reading on the sofa, with all the glass windows facing the field in front of me. It was late evening, almost dusk. And in the kitchen there was the back door with a square window facing the back garden. A service door on the back side. Usually the lights were always off outside so I could see the stars when looking out at night. The house is in the middle of nowhere, an open field, like 10 km away from a small village. No one around. That evening I was there alone as I used to be, just enjoying a book. Suddenly I saw the light of the back door turning ON, and someone knocking on the glass window of the door. I found it weird because in front of me there were the two glass walls and to reach the back door they would have to walk in front of them. Besides, the door's light switch is inside. I must say that I got stuck for a moment, trying to understand if I really heard someone knocking at the door. It couldn't be an animal like those who could be around… a wild dog, a red fox… no. It was obvious the knocking on the glass. Could be a magpie knocking on the window though. But no, the sound was softer, and the light went ON. I stood up not very enthusiastic to be honest. The energetic presence was incredibly strong, my body became very warm, my skin turned into chicken skin with my air all up. I grabbed my wooden staff, and I went to the kitchen to check what was happening…

The light outside at the top of the door was ON. And through the glass window I could see his face. A young guy, probably twelve, thirteen years old. His hair black, with no specific haircut, just with some messy bangs falling over his forehead. His head shape was like a diamond, very well cut. His skin pale almost transparent. No specific facial expression… apart from the detail of the eyes, it was just a random young teenager. But the eyes made the point: there was no white or any other colour. They were fully black. A black eyed child.

I didn't say hello and went straight to ask him "what do you want here?" His face was almost "glued" to the glass, so close it was, almost coming in through it. All this made me very apprehensive since the very beginning. I was not opened to this connection. This was the only thing I was sure of though. All the rest made me feel uneasy and confused. He was not a ghost and not a physical human. His black eyes were not black, they were deeply dark, as if they had the whole universe inside.

"Let me in…", he said softly.

"No, not now, go back home. I need some peace here." And he left. He turned his back, took two or three steps, the light went OFF again and he disappeared in that twilight before dusk.

For a long time his face remained in my memory. In fact, I still can't forget his face, as if I could see him now, and this happened six or seven years ago. His energy was also incredibly strong. Almost as paralyzing. I still don't know if I did well or not, if I regret having sent him away or not. Maybe he needed help. Maybe not. I never understood his own "agenda". And the whole universe in his eyes.

A year ago though, his image came to my mind in a very strong way, and I decided to search for something similar on internet. I had no idea that the "black eyed children" was actually a thing, seen by several other people around the world, and it seems that with exactly the same approach. "Let me in…"

There are several theories about these kind of encounters though, but none of them makes much sense to me. I still have no clue about who he was or what he wanted. Apart from the approval to let him come in. Being honest, if he would knock at my door again, I am not sure, but I will probably react the same way. Or not. It all depends on the energy I will feel at the time. But as far as I remember, his energy was like nothing I ever felt before or afterwards. And I am not sure if I am already prepared to face it. Or handle it.

One thing for sure: it was not an earthly energy as we know it.

If I will ever feel that I am ready for these encounters… I will let him know.

Science fails since it became faith. Modern science is not being innovative in any aspect, and this is mainly due to the dogmatic and conservative process. The same thing that happens with church in general. You can see the example of the Catholic church, spinning around and getting stuck in its own dogmas. Not allowing themselves to get out of itself. With science the same happens, it became a dogmatic faith. But since it has so many years of recognition, and we were always educated by it as main disciplines, we believe in science over all. In fact, there is this old saying that you either believe in institutional religion, or in institutional science.

When I had a motorbike accident on the highway out of Barcelona some years ago, I got a hernia in my spine. The ambulance came, and I decided – since I was still hot and not feeling the impact sequels much – to take my day out at the sea. At the end of the day I couldn't walk properly though. So I went to the hospital by myself for a check-up. It was clear: a hernia in my spine, between two lower vertebras. The next would be six month of therapies there while taking a bunch of pills. Those who have had a spine hernia know how it can be an "unpleasantly painful" experience for several months or even a few years.
I came back home not happy with that prognosis, so I investigated further. Physiotherapy and pills was really not a first option for me. I then found a Japanese master

operating in the area. On his website it said that he would do reiki, cupping, acupuncture, moxibustion, and energetic healing. After booking a session, I arrived a bit stressed because I was already informed about my condition, but somehow when meeting the master I felt safe. He told me to not speak, just to lie down. Checking my feet – using reflexology – he then told me that I had a hernia on those vertebras and an incredible amount of stress, and that he would need two or three sessions to heal me. I agreed, and he started by energetic healing, cupping, and then acupuncture and moxibustion. After an hour in his hands, half an hour of reiki. I know that I left there walking again, and feeling incredibly relaxed. Two more sessions followed to base the whole treatment. One hour each week for three weeks. But the fact was that after the very first one I felt healed. And this happened ten years ago, I never had to go through physiotherapy or even take pills.

What I felt was that no matter what he used, the way he used it was what healed me. It was the way he managed the energy. Like reiki. The way he played with the chi. The way he used my own energy to heal myself. Not his, or he would have become exhausted. But my own. He made me produce extra clean energy to heal myself. And that is what I use when I heal my patients: energy. Their own.

But here in this case we went even further: while he was healing me, I too was healing myself, so there was double work.

For a healing session to give its best results, you should focus on the healing and fully trust the master. Not focusing on the master as person, but trusting him, focusing on the healing itself.

Since I was a child I use energy to either make things happen or to heal others, and myself. But often I would become tired, and felt unprotected. I did not have much knowledge, and it was so natural to me that I never thought about how to improve it. I grew up a bit stuck with this, with my own dogmas. Like any religion or mainstream science. I didn't feel that looking outside and making a neutral analyses within would result in anything. Maybe science and religion by arrogance, maybe me as child in ignorance or ingenuity. But as a cultural and sociological curious person, I grew up with a diversity of interests. Reading science and different religions, sociology, philosophy, mechanics, electricity, literature and arts, music and dance, to transcendental states of being and paying attention to my own experiences in this matter of healing and mind power. How dance or spinning around can make you go into a trance. Does energy help? Is it just mechanics? And how is telepathy or even collective consciousness possible? I wanted to understand everything and more than that, what I didn't find in books. Later on I went to the Himalayas for three years. But first, I started yoga and meditation when I was thirteen years old, and transcendental meditation when I was fourteen. Later in life I learned tantra, and how we can use our own sexual source of energy to improve either physical exercise or mindful focus. I understood while feeling the meridians, the spots of energy in the body. I realized that what always made me feel so good lying down in the open field was the energetic connection with Earth, feeling the brain in the same frequency as the planet. I realized at very young age that our mind is energy, and the communication within our brain and the other between people can be just energy. Like a nervous system made of electric charges. And that is the energy that I have been always using to heal others. Their own, neutralizing mine so I can perceive and work with theirs better. Not influencing them with mine, nor absorbing theirs myself. And for this there is no ego, as there is no arrogance. There is only humbleness and gratitude.

Being a shaman, no matter from which tradition, is being connected. Connected with the Earth, its plants and wisdom, animals, and living beings in general. Connected also with cosmic awareness, universe and its own energy, and aware of its events. It is being one with all beings, nature and cosmos. With the spirits of nature and the wisdom of universe. It is being aware of life.
And when you obtain this level, you became free of ego, you become wiser.

When you reach the level of consciousness, when you become fully aware of this energy, you can go into trance by ordering your mind as you order your hand to go up or go down. You order your patient's energy to heal itself. To recycle. Without the need of pills. Nature gives us all we need to heal ourselves and others. We are the Earth, on the same level of energy as the plants and animals and any other being.

And here science fails again with its dogmatic posture as they refuse to acknowledge that there's more than just matter. That it is energy that is playing the bigger or higher role. Not all is mechanical or matter, and that is why for example science is so late with understanding how the brain works. The brain is mostly energy connecting itself. And it is the brain's energy, that in connection to consciousness creates the mind. The consciousness that is only made of energy. And that exists everywhere. Yes, dear scientists, stones have energy and consciousness too. They are not just matter. They have as much consciousness as each of us have. Working on the same frequency of Earth, connecting to the universe through its own vibration and sound.

Let the energy flow and be aware of how wise it is.

For now, don't worry about science (or religion), as one day soon, science will understand that, like gravity, consciousness is part of the whole, it connects all and it is everywhere. This is not a new concept, in fact, in the western world it has a name: Panpsychism.

In philosophy, panpsychism is the view that consciousness, mind or soul (psyche) is a universal and primordial feature of all things. Panpsychists see themselves as consciousness in a world of consciousness.

But then, this comes from ancient times.

Panpsychism is one of the oldest philosophical theories, and has been ascribed to philosophers like Plato, Spinoza and Leibniz. Panpsychism can also be seen in ancient philosophies like Mahayana Buddhism.

During the 19th century, panpsychism was the default theory in philosophy of mind, but it saw a decline during the middle years of the 20th century with the rise of logical thinking, with the mainstream of modern science. The one that got stuck in its own dogmatic arrogance, following the institutional religion.

Δ

Mind power is a whole connection within oneself and the universe. It is all about higher consciousness of the self. When I went through brain death, I used mind power, high consciousness, going through transcendental meditation and ordering my heart to stop feeding my brain with oxygen. This requires silence of mind, mind power and higher consciousness. However, the process is quite simple. If I tell you to raise your right hand, your mind will automatically inform your hand to rise up. And in a moment you have your hand up. The same process goes with our internal organs. The main thing here is that you grew up becoming aware only of the exterior of the body. The moment you decide to stand up and walk, your mind sends an energetic and magnetic impulse that makes your legs move. It is the same rule. If you visualize the inner organ in your body and inform it to do a specific action, it will do it. While I was in the Sahara, I ate a bit of food that had garlic and I was not aware of it. I'm very allergic to garlic, and it can kill me in a few hours. I am aware of this, and in fact I never tried to heal this energy because I find garlic to be poison for our system and I don't like either its texture, smell or taste. So I keep the allergy, to inform me that I have been poisoned. That moment though I couldn't do anything but heal. The moment I became aware of the garlic, my throat was already bloating inside and my breath became more difficult. I immediately focused on the garlic inside my body and informed the body to expel the garlic's energy. I was having a meal with some friends, and I didn't want to go through dramas, vomiting, etc. so I focused, visualized the garlic, became aware of its energy, and expelled it. They were looking at me and understood what happened, so they remained silent observing me. The moment I ordered the energy of the garlic to come out, it was still located in the esophagus, but already close to the stomach. I was wearing a few chains with pendants from several cultures that I often use. That moment all the pendants just jumped, and when they come back to their natural position, hanging over my chest, my breath became normal again. I expelled the garlic's energy that was causing me the allergy.

This is the same thing that I do to heal my patients, no matter if I'm in a real meeting or through a webcam, when they live abroad. I visualize their issues, turn them into energy and free the patient of the issue's energy, expelling it or transforming it. Sometimes it requires more than a few steps. When I healed the patient with cancer, I transformed the tumour into a stone, and only then could I expel the stone with its own energy.

Δ

Talking with other shamans from different traditions and all kind of stages, I realized that there are two main worries amongst them. One being "how to keep ourselves protected from other's energies" and "how to go in trance faster and deeper".

First of all, put one thing in your mind. Inform your mind about this:

Life is not happening to you: Life is responding to you!

And life is consciousness. Your own consciousness, connected to the collective consciousness, part of the cosmic consciousness. It is all an incredible and intricate system of energy.

When you think "I hate when I feel my energy being drained by others" or "I don't know why can't I protect myself from others", life, or consciousness will answer you with what you sent to it "hate" "delusion" "anxiety" and "weakness".

However, when you silence your mind and become neutral and focused on positivity, life will respond to you in the same manner, giving you silence, awareness, love, peace, skills, strength. And trust. Trust, because you become aware of your positivity, your peace and silence that brings you wise consciousness to deal with whatever you need.

If you don't trust, if you're anxious, if you have any

negative thoughts, it is better to stay away from other people, even less trying to heal them, as you might send them your energy.

First of all go into silence. And by this I mean: get rid of your ego. Get rid of yourself. Be energy, be connected and one with your own consciousness. Be silence, and be peace. This is enough to keep your own strength and produce even more healing energy. You can do it, don't doubt. You can do it. Trust yourself.

Be consciousness, because it is consciousness that is over mind. Mind sometimes plays tricks, so it's better to always focus and trust consciousness, or intuition, as you might call it. Mind can be rational and sometimes fake. Intuition does not fail if you listen to it properly.

If you like pure transparent water, you don't add coffee to it. You all know that coffee will not only change the colour and purity of the clear water, but will also awaken your brain with caffeine. Coffee is the brain awakening the mind. Think of consciousness as white pure water from the sacred mountains. Clear crystal pure water that you can trust. Now don't forget that your body is mainly water. And frequency, in the same resonance of the Earth.

How wonderful we are! How grateful we all should be.

The moment you become aware of your consciousness, and how it is connected to the collective and cosmic consciousness, the easier it will become for you to control your mind. To have Mind Power. Mind power is being awakened, aware of our own consciousness. In silence. In peace. Being able to heal yourself and others. Sharing and spreading awareness through this energetic consciousness. Think focused. Think positivity. Clear crystal thoughts. Direct your focus on trust. On peace. On healing. Be crystal. Be water. Be pure.

When you reach this, you just need to inform your mind to shut down, and use the consciousness to go into silence, into trance, into your own healing tool. In a single click. You are the only one who can chose if the mind switch is OFF, or ON. And when it is ON, you are awakened, silent, able to heal, to connect, to be crystal clear and pure consciousness.

Δ

Practice silence in your daily life. Whenever you have five minutes, sit down and focus on silence. You may carry with you a stone, a pebble, a magnet, a colourful gem or a crystal, if it helps you.

Focus on it whenever you have a moment. While you are waiting for the food; or taking the train. It doesn't matter, whenever you have few moments, instead of being negatively absorbing the surroundings, take the stone out of your pocket and focus on it. Find its own silence, connect, and find your own silence. By doing this, you are not only awakening yourself, producing self-awareness, finding silence… and eventually spreading it through others.
Practice this simple action daily, at different moments of the day. Make it your secret daily ritual. With short practice you will soon become more aware. Breath in and out. Focus on your inhale and exhale. Focus on the pebble. Connect with it. Find the silence. Silence your mind. Be consciousness. Spread that silence. Fulfil yourself.
Be one with nature. Allow yourself to shift.
This will give power and strength to your own consciousness. Your consciousness will bring to you more awareness, making you more awakened. Allow Consciousness to work its own anamnesis, building your own true self.
Being One.

Δ

Love